Over Forty at Last

How to Avoid the "Mid-life Crisis" and Make the Most of the Best Years of Your Life

Over Forty at Last

by Susanna Kubelka

MACMILLAN PUBLISHING CO., INC.
NEW YORK

Translated by Allegra Branson

Macmillan Publishing Co., Inc.
866 Third Avenue, New York, N.Y. 10022
Collier Macmillan Canada, Inc.

Library of Congress Cataloging in Publication Data
Kubelka, Susanna, 1942–
    Over forty at last.
    Translation of: Endlich über vierzig.
    1. Middle aged women—Psychology. I. Title.
HQ1059.4.K8213   305.2′44   82-15369
ISBN 0-02-567150-2   AACR2

10 9 8 7 6 5 4 3 2 1

Printed in the United States of America

To my mother, who has given me life and, better still, taught me the joy of living.

Contents

Introduction

We live in a strange world. On the one hand we are more prosperous than ever before; on the other, instead of enjoying what we have got, we devote most of our energies to the task of making ourselves miserable. Everyone seems to be afraid of something and, if we don't watch it, our age will go down in history as the Age of Anxiety.

It seems ridiculous, and nobody quite knows why it's true, but in the last forty years men, and especially women, have let themselves be submerged by crisis after crisis. You name it: postnatal depression, premenstrual syndrome, midlife crisis, empty-nest syndrome . . . and before long there will be more. People are already talking (and writing) about the "Monday morning syndrome" and soon we shall all be left shattered by postbreakfast and preluncheon shock. I suppose we shall only finally be satisfied when, from dusk to dawn, from cradle to grave, we can happily wallow in crisis after crisis and not have to worry about life anymore.

And this is precisely where the question of age comes in. All the time we are reminded of it—and until about two years ago most allusions to age were negative. What makes matters worse, perfectly well-balanced people have let themselves be brainwashed into believing that fears of growing older are absolutely necessary, that there is a crisis at every step, that it is part of the human condition to experience at least some kind of midlife melancholy.

This, of course, is nonsense. Look at Europeans. To them, growing up and becoming a mature person has always been something to strive for. To develop on command a state of anxiety in the prime of your life (and waste a lot of time by doing so) is considered ridiculous. If you ask a Frenchwoman about her midlife crisis, she won't even know what you are talking about. As a matter of fact, the French have not even found it necessary to translate the term into their own language.

Personally, I know a lot of people, men as well as women, who sail through life gloriously, never wasting a thought on fashionable gloom, genuinely enjoying themselves as they get older. I have met them everywhere, all over the world through my career as a journalist and writer, and every day their number seems to be increasing.

Doing research for this book has rid me of the last shred of doubt: Times are really changing and they are changing in favor of the mature person.

Never before have we all stayed young so long. Never before have women been so successful in careers, made so much money, or taken so many young lovers. To me, of course, this is nothing new. I come from a happy family where nobody ever made a fuss about growing older. My mother married in her early thirties and was forty-two when I was born. Today, she is a high-spirited eighty-two and we really enjoy each other's company.

My grandmother was in her mid-seventies when she married her third husband, a young man of twenty. They were blissfully happy for a whole decade until she died at the age of eighty-six. She was an irresistible woman. My great uncle Edmund, after having traveled the world, decided at age sixty to start a family, which he promptly did. Even apart from my relatives, I have known a great many fascinating older women as positive role models, women who have proved to me that life is indeed worth living and that the date on your birth certificate is totally insignificant.

No wonder that the subject of growing older has intrigued me all my life. From the age of eighteen on I kept a diary, observed people critically, asked a lot of questions, and recorded faithfully everything that struck me as interesting. I have read as much as I could find on the subject of growing up, growing older, becoming a mature person, living a long and fulfilled life. I have also done a lot of research on earlier centuries. I was forced to do this in order to write a dissertation on English women novelists of the eighteenth century, but soon I got so involved that, after three years of work, I found it painful to stop.

To write this book, I compared my notes on the past to those on the present. And, believe me, the tidings are good. The world no longer belongs to the very young—as a matter of fact, it never did! The world, as we shall soon prove, belongs to people with maturity, personality, character, and experience. Stop feeling uneasy about your age. The world is yours for the taking. If you read this book, you will never worry about growing older again.

Over Forty at Last

1

Why Are We Afraid of Age?

I am forty years old and I have never felt better in my life. I enjoy my age and I am looking forward to adding to it. All those fears that made my twenties miserable have vanished. I finally know what getting older means: It means, most of all, change, and I thrive on it. It means moving around, living in new houses and apartments, learning about foreign countries, speaking new languages, meeting a lot of new and interesting people. Best of all, it means getting nearer to finally being able to figure out what life is all about.

I never enjoyed being young. I was miserable at school. I found my classmates uninteresting, silly, and even malicious, and my teachers did not do much for me either. As for men, I hated those dubious compliments they paid me as I passed them on the street. Walking by a construction site on my way to school and listening to what the workers had to say was agony. If being young was supposed to be enjoyable, I missed something. My first love affairs and sexual experiences were disasters. I had no money, no self-confidence, and no idea what I should do with my life. I have much more fun now, at forty, than I had as a teenager. I would never want to be twenty again!

Throughout the entire Western world, there is an unnatural, almost morbid fear of growing older. Any mention of the word "old" . . . and people start to panic. Men and women have forgotten that it is possible to age gracefully, that maturity is something to look forward to. The Chinese, however, don't celebrate birthdays until they reach seventy. "Children's birthdays are cheap," they say. "Everybody starts off as an infant. So where is the merit?" Compare this to our own shaky sense of self: We kowtow to the young, we behave as if the blossom were better than the fruit, and we cheapen ourselves in the process.

The people who are most afraid of getting older are frequently those who have never had any real contact with the elderly. In Europe, fortunately, many of us had a grandparent or even a great-grandparent living at home, and thus we learned firsthand that people do not change that much with age, that they can remain graceful and elegant, lively and humorous, and enjoy life up to their dying day.

A lot of people thrive on self-destruction. There are two sides to everything, and we pride ourselves on our ability to see the negative side only. We are never happy with our age. If we are young we want to be older. If we are older we want to be young. Instead of liking what we've got, instead of enjoying the fact that we are *just* thirty, forty, fifty, or sixty, we complain about *already* being twenty-five, forty-three, or sixty-nine.

Well, everybody is welcome to cheapen himself or herself, but nobody has the right to make others miserable, to undermine their healthy self-esteem or their high spirits by asserting that nothing good ever happens to anyone over thirty and that, at forty-five, there's nothing left to do except to sell out to the younger generation.

As much as I like and esteem men, I can't help saying that they are in great measure responsible for this. Because they have attached too much importance to their sexual potency and have worried so about losing it, they have talked themselves into a frenzy, with the result that grown men are now afraid of mere schoolboys because they think that they can make love more often. I do hope men will soon realize how ridiculous this is. What good to a woman is a lover who has ten orgasms a night after sixty seconds of lovemaking? Give me a mature man any time, a man who has control over his body, a man who will take his time. Any sensible woman knows that in lovemaking it is the quality and not the quantity that counts!

But what I am much more unhappy about is the fact that men have for centuries projected their own fear of aging onto their wives and mistresses. Because they were scared and did not want to admit it, they skilfully convinced their women that it was *they* who have everything to lose and nothing to gain, that it was *the women* who really ought to dread growing older, because nobody would want them, touch them, feed them, look after them, once the first wrinkles began to show. And for generations women were too dependent emotionally and economically to defend themselves.

Now, let's forget for a moment all the propaganda. Why should women be more afraid of aging than men are? Biologically, there is no reason. Women do not become impotent. Women do not lose their hair. Women stay fertile most of their adult lives, usually until they reach their early fifties. My mother did not reach menopause until she was fifty-eight—and don't forget my grandmother!

Women also get fewer wrinkles than men. Exercise, a proper diet, cosmetics, stimulating work, and outside interests can keep a woman looking attractive and sexy well

5

into her seventies. But however she looks, in our day and age she is able to feed herself. And this is the most important argument of all.

I find it difficult to understand why modern women are so afraid of age. There is no historical precedent for this fear. In all the great European and Asian cultures, it was the mature woman and never the girl who was revered. Ovid, the Roman expert on love and sexuality, wrote that a woman did not even begin to develop until she was thirty-six. Women, not girls, were worshiped and desired during the Middle Ages, the Renaissance, and well into the first half of the eighteenth century.

Let's take a look into seventeenth-century Parisian society. *Ninon de Lenclos* was not the only "older woman" to be surrounded by admirers and lovers up to her dying day. Respected by all and showered with honors, she was described by one poet as "aging exquisitely, as a rose spreads its petals. . . ." She lived to be ninety.

Another example from the same epoch: *Anne Geneviève de Bourbon,* later Countess of Longueville, was universally recognized as the most beautiful woman in Paris. You know how old she was when this title was bestowed upon her? She was fifty!

Many a modern woman's hysterical reaction to aging would be quickly dispelled were she exposed to the accounts of the lives and conquests of many other Parisian ladies of the seventeenth and eighteenth centuries—*Madame de Lafayette, Madame de Sévigné, La Grande Mademoiselle* (daughter of Gaston, Duke of Orleans), *Mademoiselle de Scudéry,* to name only a few of the most well known. Mature women were admired in Spain, Italy, Germany, Switzerland, and Austria as well as in France. *Lady Wortley-Montague,* famous for her lively letters and travel anecdotes, once stopped over in Vienna en route to join her husband, the English ambassador to Turkey. On September 20, 1716, she wrote to her friend Lady Rich in London: "Let me assure you, dear, the Viennese women let neither gray hair nor stooped shoulders get in the way of making new conquests. Every day I see handsome young men helping their much older lovers into their coaches. In this worldly capital, women under thirty-five are regarded as immature. A woman can't even hope to make a lasting impression on people until she's over forty."

Given this tradition, isn't it all the more curious that in the nineteenth century unmarried women were "old maids" at twenty-five? Even today, a woman who has her first child at thirty is described as coming "late" to motherhood. What happened between the eighteenth and nineteenth centuries to produce so drastic a change in attitude?

The Industrial Revolution began in England during the first half of the eighteenth century and lasted for about seventy years. During this time, a middle class emerged, whose existence was spawned by the new money generated by factory-produced goods. Up to that time there had been only two classes in England: the aristocracy and the peasantry. This new "middle" class needed large families (power in numbers) to survive and secure its place in the rather rigid British class system. This was only possible if women devoted themselves solely to childbearing and rearing, and left affairs of the world to the men who ordered their lives.

Thus, in the eighteenth century, a woman very different from her forebears emerged in England. This creature—faithful, domestic, obedient—produced, without a murmur, astonishing numbers of children and was subservient to her husband in nearly every way.

By the middle of the eighteenth century writers, theologians, politicians, and philosophers sang the virtues of this image of woman in choral unison. In plays, newspapers, Sunday sermons, and the popular novels of the day, good women all fit into this one mold. Their preachers, teachers, journalists, fathers, and beaux asserted that women should not strive for love nor for physical or intellectual fulfillment. Indeed not, because the only true and "holy" womanly attributes were self-denial, obedience, chastity, fidelity, and devotion to children, husband, and domesticity.

To keep women in check, men emphasized the transitory quality of feminine beauty. The bloom of youth was brief, they said (and wrote and preached). Age or some horrible sickness might rob a marriageable woman of youth before she knew what had hit her. Novels were forbidden reading filled with despicable male characters: unfaithful lovers, white-slave dealers, and rapists. A "good" woman could follow only one road to salvation, and there was only one safe haven on that road: the arms of a husband. In the same novels, the husbands, women's true saviors, were pictured as men of unparalleled virtue. Only they were able to save helpless women from dishonor or rape, from lives botched by loneliness, uselessness, and the ridicule that society heaped on an "old maid."

How could these tactics fail? By the beginning of the nineteenth century the image of the typical woman had been drastically recast. It was as if nature had reversed itself, turning the witty, educated, and admired society butterfly of the salon into a pale, virtuous, continuously pregnant and sickly domestic. Married too early, a woman never had time to test her wings. Her sexual life was over before it began. Her only source of power in a society that denied her both education and a career had been her sexual attractiveness, and now she was denied even that. She had little determination or will to live, and she aged quickly.

Nonetheless, men, still fearful that women might develop an interest in sex and sensuality that would threaten men's newly attained domestic bliss, went to great lengths to shield women from any literature that might arouse romantic emotions or erotic desire. While early eighteenth-century men and women giggled together over erotic scenes in books and plays, by the end of that same century sexuality had disappeared underground and literature could be divided into two categories: "clean" family books for women and children, and pornography for men. Early in the nineteenth century, fifty-nine pornographic bookstores opened practically overnight in London's Holywell Street. Meanwhile, even Shakespeare's works were purged of suggestive words that could not be read in a family setting "without offending the delicacy of women."

It's no wonder that the nineteenth-century woman, repressed and in poor health from continuous childbearing, worried about getting old. The short years between childhood and marriage, where she was allowed to flirt, dance, and display her charms, truly were the best years of her life. As the nineteenth century proceeded, girls were married off at younger and younger ages so that they might produce even more children and avoid the temptations of a healthy sex life altogether. The new fear of growing old and the changed image of women made its way from England into the former colonies and there, in North America, the celebration of Youth soon became a tradition. But not for the reason you think.

The United States did not win independence until the latter part of the eighteenth century. The Wild West had to be conquered, and life on the frontier was pitiless:

Women and men worked like slaves side by side and death came early to many. A lot of newborn babies died, and this, in my opinion, is the underlying reason for the exaggerated North American youth cult—not, as we shall see, the supposition that women in such harsh times wore out fast.

If you read about pioneer women and the amount of work they did while still living in dugouts or on their farms, if you picture their crossing the Rocky Mountains, eight or nine months pregnant, giving birth in rainstorms and blizzards, you'll soon realize how well these women bore up. And, once settled, they started schools, hospitals, libraries, churches, and even theaters after having raised their children.

Try to find books about the lives of some of the early women missionaries (they were all married) or, as a contrast, about some of the famous courtesans who, like *Julia Bulette*, in Comstock Lode, earned up to a thousand dollars a day for her favors.

No, it was certainly not the frailty of those women that sparked off the glorification of the young. It was the desperate need for children to preserve the society, and the fact that children in those early days had a hard time surviving. There is a very moving episode recounted in a Time-Life book on western women (gorgeous photographs and fascinating text by Joan Swallow-Reiter) about a crowd of people congregating in a small, makeshift theater somewhere in the west to watch a play. A woman had brought a small child with her, and the child began to cry during the performance. And you know what happened? Everyone was delighted. "Stop the show," an old man yelled at the top of his voice, "stop the show so that we can all hear the baby cry!"

On top of the struggle to preserve frontier society, a

struggle that brought about the glorification of everything that is young and fresh, Americans developed a horror of dying. The United States, being a young country, had a much more difficult time accepting the phenomenon of death than did older European or Asian societies, which had taught themselves ages earlier how to come to terms with it. These older cultures have had time to get used to the idea that life is not eternal. In China, Japan, and India, to name only a few, death is an accepted, even honored end to our existence.

In the United States, however, most people are terrified of dying. They have enjoyed the good life and a high standard of living for only a few generations, and they want to keep it all for as long as possible. Most of the wealth still belongs to men—and because a woman's financial and social status has traditionally depended on her husband's, women have dreaded aging even more than their male counterparts. This insecurity has been excerbated by the fairly common practice among many American men of exercising what they have deemed their right—to trade in their first wives, usually contemporaries, for younger models, believing that a young wife will delay their own aging. Is it any wonder then that American women, as recently as fifteen years ago, were horrified at even the slightest sign of age? How can we blame women who suspected, often with good reason, that the threat of divorce and the resulting financial and social deprivation lay behind every admiring glance their husbands gave younger-looking females? How hard can we be, in all fairness, on the fifty-year-old woman who wears ribbons in her dyed or bleached hair and speaks in a childish voice? Women posing in one form or another as children is, after all, a time-honored tradition by now.

The writer Anaïs Nin, who fled Paris for the United

States during World War II, wrote, "Just as we were beginning to enjoy the advantages of our prime, we were forced to leave Europe for a country that worships only youth and immaturity."

In 1945, the American Army of Occupation in Europe brought with it the American fixation on youth. At first Europeans shrugged it off, particularly the women who had demonstrated their own capabilities by filling the jobs left vacant by the men at the front. They thought it absurd to believe that they would be tossed out on the junk heap because of a few superficial wrinkles on their faces. But gradually the American reverence for youth infected them, too. Although the youth cult has never been quite as pervasive on the Continent as it has been in the States and in England, the European woman's self-confidence was nonetheless dealt a painful blow.

Another postwar phenomenon, the maturing American film industry, played a substantial role in entrenching the cult of youth. Suddenly, only the very young seemed to have a right to live. Older, accomplished women, women of achievement and character, were rarely featured. The silver screen idolized only the smooth complexions of the young, their trusting cowlike eyes, and above all their willingness to forego education and careers for wedded bliss and the careful maintenance of rose-covered cottages. In the late 1940s, 1950s, and 1960s, it seemed that the mission of the Hollywood film studios was to push American females into marriage and motherhood as early as the law would permit to replenish the population lost in the war.

During this period, the mature woman was not in an enviable position. She had few desirable role models, and age became her enemy, although she knew she was more capable, accomplished, and interesting than she had been as a young girl. Little did it do for her. When the veterans returned to their jobs, the women who had "filled in" for them returned to being housewives, a role taken for granted and often depicted condescendingly. Television, which came of age during this period in the United States, became the logical dispenser of the popular values and myths surrounding the mass retreat of women from offices and factories to the nest. The 1950s was not a time for throwing too bright a light on the misfortunes of the poor or elderly, but rather a period dedicated to repairing and uplifting the middle class, as its men returned from fighting overseas to their families. If the husbands and fathers depicted in such popular offerings as "Father Knows Best" and "Leave It to Beaver" were exemplary providers and repositories of wisdom, the wives and mothers were saints: the perfect nurturers, helpmates, and demurely sexy live-in maids. The degree to which such women were judged "good" depended almost entirely (as it had a century earlier) on the degree to which she served others, knowing her place and not deviating from it, deferring with winning childlike simplicity to the worldliness of he who "knows best."

So much for a short summary of how women have changed over the past two centuries and why they have suddenly developed an unnatural fear of aging. We have seen how society's view of women made a 180-degree turn from a time when elegant, often gray-haired ladies were surrounded by younger lovers and admirers to our own time, when many a forty-five-year-old housewife considers herself undesirable, useless, and a little over the hill.

I also hope that this summary has convinced you that the fear of growing older is a very short-lived phenomenon. Let's never forget the basic truth: There is no particular merit in being young. The young of today are no longer threatened by disease and poverty as they were in the Old West (or the New East). Practically all babies survive into childhood now. So, what is so special about youth? If you are born into this world, you necessarily start off young. But to be young is not an end in itself. Life was not given to us for the sole purpose of flaunting a smooth face and an empty head for the rest of our days. To be a pretty teenager is fine—but it is no achievement. The real purpose of being born is to grow up, to become a mature, knowledgeable human being, to develop a personality, and then—full speed ahead with all you've got!

However, be patient. Don't be upset if you have not found your purpose in life by the time you are twenty or twenty-five. The longer we live, the longer we take to grow up. If you are a late bloomer—all the better. You'll last twice as long!

Never forget that people are different. Talents and capabilities don't develop automatically at a certain age. You have to find your own pattern—you have to wait until *you* are ready. Once you know that, you're all right.

Some people reach their highest level of accomplishment at twenty and never develop much beyond that point. But those are a minority. Others are fifty before they know what their talents are and what they can or can't do. Whatever age you are, it's never too late to change direction, start something new, or do something you've always dreamed of doing. "I'm too old for that" is not an objective assessment but usually an excuse to remain in a comfortable niche and not risk failure. Material considerations and opportunities may vary, but age is no excuse. Nobody is too old to go back to school at fifty or to change his life at sixty. It's not the chronological age that counts but the willingness to make the effort and take the risk.

If the will is strong enough, you can do just about anything.

14

Why haven't we heard more about outstanding women through the years, or even today with our mass media? Just one example is often enough to give the rest of us that needed incentive to jump up and do something ourselves. There are hundreds of thousands of women who have been active and productive as long as they were able to breathe. A few examples, not to cause any envy but to spur us on, help to remind us that fulfillment and success are indeed within our reach.

In the 1950s, just as the youth cult was at its height, an American woman named *Anna Mary Moses* made headlines. To art historians she became "Grandma Moses." She was a simple farm wife who rarely traveled far from her home in upstate New York, but at the age of seventy-five she decided to take up painting.

At first she painted in the same traditional style that you can see in just about any American museum, but she soon developed her own unique approach, unleashing a flood of so-called naïve painting. Unaware that she was working toward a breakthrough art form that had been rejected up until then, she simply painted her surroundings as she saw them and was surprised to find how well her work sold. Soon her style was being imitated by other artists whose works helped fill American and European galleries as well as the pockets of countless art dealers. But hardly any of her imitators reached the artistic perfection of her work.

Although her paintings commanded astonishing prices even in her lifetime, Anna Mary Moses wasn't interested in fame or in appearances. She only wanted to find an outlet for her creative energy, and she succeeded. She died in 1961, famous and contented at the age of 101.

Lesson: Even at the age of eighty or older a woman can make her mark on life if she is determined to do so.

15

Speaking of women painters, you can look back through the centuries and find any number of women who remained creative all their lives. And most of them lived to a very old age. It is not true that twentieth-century men, and women, live that much longer than their ancestors. Only now are we beginning to find out that those statistics compiled for past centuries are deceptive because the high rate of infant mortality has been taken into account and lowered, on paper, everyone's lifespan. (Johann Sebastian Bach, for example, had more than twenty children, of whom only ten lived to maturity.) In those former days, if you survived childhood diseases and, in the case of young adult women, childbirth itself, you stood a good chance of living to a ripe old age. And why shouldn't you?

The air then was cleaner, the food untainted by chemicals; streams and rivers ran unpolluted by industrial waste. Sure, they had their incurable diseases, but we have our car accidents. They had no cure for tuberculosis; we have no cure for heart disease or cancer. In studying the biographies of great men and women of the past, you might be astonished to see how many of them, women in particular, lived to be eighty, ninety, and even older.

The famous English bluestockings, or blues, in the eighteenth century are a perfect illustration of this point. At school we were fed horror stories about the eighteenth-century lack of medical knowledge, poor personal hygiene, and filthy city streets—and yet look at these figures:

Elegant *Elizabeth Montagu,* the "Queen of the Blues," lived to be eighty. Writer *Hester Thrale,* mother of twelve, lived to be eighty-one. Novelist *Fanny (Frances) Burney* lived to be eighty-eight years old, as did poet and moralist *Hannah More,* and the very beautiful, widely admired writer, *Mary Delany,* lived to eighty-nine. *Elizabeth Carter,* a renowned Greek scholar saw her ninety-second birthday, and *Mary Monckton,* celebrated London hostess and later known as "the last of the blues," lived ninety-four long years.

You've probably never heard of many of these women, yet in their day they were outstanding artists, writers, and painters—and all remained creative *throughout* their long lives.

Gisela of Bavaria was the sister of Emperor Henry II. She was born in A.D. 980 and was married at the age of fifteen, for reasons of state, to Stephen I, who became the patron saint of Hungary. She became famous for her needlework, among her creations an ecclesiastical garment that was later incorporated into the coronation coat of the Hungarian kings. After her husband died, Gisela entered a convent, which was the only proper place for a single lady of her time. She spent the rest of her life crafting beautiful designs and died at the age of eighty.

Hildegard of Bingen lived about one hundred years later. She was a Benedictine nun, founded the Rupertsberg convent, and was universally regarded as a genius. People said she was endowed with prophetic gifts. Whether that is so or not, she did teach and publish works on poetry, music, medicine, and natural history. She spoke several languages and carried on a lively correspondence with emperors, kings, popes, and cardinals—in short, with the important European rulers of her time. She illustrated one of her books with thirty-five gold-and-silver paintings that were so unusual experts spoke of her "revolutionary" painting technique. Hildegard lived to be eighty-one and was made a saint by the Church.

Tommasina da Fiesco lived during the fifteenth century in Genoa. Widowed early in life, she entered a convent and soon became renowned as both a writer and creator

17

of fine needlework. Later, she invented tempera painting, a technique that is widely used today. Tommasina lived to be eighty-six years old and was creative all her life.

The Italian painter *Sofonisba Anguussola* was another fascinating personality. She was regarded by none other than the Flemish artist Anthony Van Dyck as the most important woman painter of her time. She was her own woman, was respected by princes and kings, and eventually accepted an invitation from Philip II of Spain to visit his court at Madrid. She remained there for twenty years as portraitist to the royal family.

Sofonisba married for the first time at age forty-five. Her husband was a Sicilian and took her off to live with him in Palermo. When he died, she married the captain of the ship that had brought her to Sicily from Spain. Van Dyck continued to admire her work so much that he visited her in Palermo and made several sketches of her. The "divine" Sofonisba lived to be ninety.

And what of the great ladies of France? *Louise Moillon,* a Parisian painter of the seventeenth century, created works regarded as some of the most important examples of the French still-life genre. This lady married at the age of thirty and lived to be sixty-eight.

[Marie Anne] *Elisabeth Vigée-Lebrun*—next to Angelica Kauffmann the most famous woman painter of the eighteenth century—lived to be eighty-seven. She was an intimate friend of Marie Antoinette, and, if her self-portrait is true to life, she was very beautiful indeed. She published her memoirs at the age of eighty-two.

Elisabeth was a great favorite with her contemporaries. Forced to flee France during the French Revolution, she was warmly welcomed at the royal courts of Russia, Italy, and England, and this royal patronage saw her overwhelmed with commissions. Some eight hundred pictures comprise her legacy, among them exquisite examples of eighteenth-century portraiture.

Two of the most famous women artists of the nineteenth century were the American *Mary Cassatt* and the Austrian *Tina Blau.* Cassatt became well known as an Impressionist, Blau as a landscape artist. Cassatt lived to be eighty-two; Blau ninety-two years.

Why have we heard so little of these long-lived creative women? German painter *Hannah Hoech* lived to be eighty-nine, Swedish painter *Vera Nilsson* ninety-one. The expatriate American *Romaine Brooks* lived to be ninety-three, as did American photographer *Imogene Cunningham,* who, shortly before her death, completed a series of portraits of people over the age of ninety; some of these works were exhibited at the American cultural center in Paris in 1977. Cunningham was also the first woman to photograph naked men, and she did so with the same attention to detail that men had used in their studies of women. She experimented with her art to the very end.

So who is afraid of getting older? Does the image of the fragile mimosa begin to fade when set against these women who embodied so ably the spirit of enterprise, lust for life, and creativity?

We know the names of history's famous creative women, and we know the titles of some of their works as well, but it's not very often we know at what period in their lives they were their most creative.

Swedish novelist *Selma Lagerlöf* was forty-eight when she wrote the children's classic, *The Wonderful Adventures of Nils,* and she was fifty-one when she was awarded the Nobel Prize.

The eighteenth-century English writer *Frances Trollope* was a dutiful housewife and mother until she was forty-seven, when she suddenly realized she had an overwhelming desire for adventure. At that point in her life, when nobody expected anything further from her, she decided to travel to America. In those days it was a bit more complicated than hopping on the nearest airplane. The ship's voyage took several weeks; the crossings were expensive, uncomfortable, and dangerous.

But, once she arrived in New York, she used her meager savings to set up a lending library and began to write. At the age of fifty she returned to London, where her book about the lifestyles and mores of Americans became an immediate best-seller. Not content with her accomplishments, she turned out forty-one more books and became the darling of London society before she died.

Another example: *George Eliot,* whose real name was Marian Evans. She lived in the nineteenth century and published her first novel at the age of forty. Her greatest success and her finest novel, *Middlemarch,* came later, published when George Eliot was fifty-three.

Now, let's switch to the United States. The great American writer *Edith Wharton* was another woman who achieved literary fame after the age of forty. (And commercial success on top of it!) Her greatest novels, *The House of Mirth, Ethan Frome,* and *The Age of Innocence* were published between her forty-third and fifty-eighth year. When she was sixty, in 1922, she received the Pulitzer Prize. From that time until her death at the age of seventy-five she completed a number of brilliant short stories, twelve more novels, and an autobiography—all the while traveling widely and leading an active social life!

British writer *Enid Bagnold,* author of *National Velvet,* was over fifty when her first play was produced based on her novel. Her greatest success was *The Chalk Garden,* which opened when she was fifty-eight. Another smash hit, based on her book *The Chinese Prime Minister,* opened when she was sixty-three. And do you know what Bagnold had printed on the jacket of her autobiography? A quote from one of her plays. It reads: "To be old is *magnificent!*"

In more recent times, there are numerous examples of older women coming into their own. *Katharine Graham* was forty-six years old when her husband suddenly died. Philip Graham had been president of the *Washington Post.* Despite all opposition, skepticism, and doubts as to her ability, Katharine Graham took over the paper and continued her husband's work. Fifteen years later, at the age of sixty-one, she had become the chairman of the board of *Newsweek,* publisher of *Artnews,* and owner of several radio and television stations.

Turning to show business: One immediately thinks of *Mary Pickford,* the queen of silent films, who was fifty-two years old when she founded her own movie company, Pickford Productions, Inc. This was her second such venture. An earlier concern, which she ran together with her husband, actor Douglas Fairbanks, comedian Charlie Chaplin, and D. W. Griffith, became a worldwide success: United Artists.

Let's stay with show business for a while. Some think this is mainly a youth-oriented realm. But it isn't. Show biz belongs to the hard worker, to the genuinely talented, to those with experience and personality—and age is an advantage. A large number of mature women are making it on stage right under our very eyes. First of all *Lena Horne,* world-famous jazz singer, and her sold-out one-woman show on Broadway in 1981. Lena had New York at her feet, with the critics raving, swearing that she was at the top of her form at age sixty-three! She received a special Tony Award, and through her brilliant performance has helped to soothe *our* silly fears of growing older.

Another sensational woman is *Lauren Bacall,* who proves that fifty-eight in our day and age is young. She scored a smash hit with her musical *Woman of the Year,* for which she won a Tony Award.

Of course, one must not forget *Katharine Hepburn,* who is in her seventies, and her Broadway play—not to mention her starring role in the film *On Golden Pond*—and the comeback of fifty-two-year-old *Joanne Woodward,* (Paul Newman's wife) who opened in 1981 in a revival of *Candida.*

So far we have four women ranging in age from fifty-two to seventy-four delighting everybody, taking New York by storm, sweeping this sophisticated audience off its feet through their brilliant performances. And if you think four is not enough, there's *Ann Miller,* famous for those long, perfect legs that have lost none of their appeal since they danced up a storm in many movies in the forties and fifties. Those legs are filling the house right now, as you can see from the overwhelming success of her performance in the musical *Sugar Babies.* Ann Miller is nearly sixty.

So what have we got? Five great women over fifty, singing, dancing, acting on the stages of Broadway theaters night after night, being rewarded with standing ovations and industry awards. Who wants to be twenty again?

If Americans taught the rest of the world to be afraid of getting older, Americans are now leading the way to overcoming these fears. *Betty Friedan,* the well-known feminist and founder of the National Organization for Women, described a new "four-dimensional woman" in her book *It Changed My Life* (Random House, New York, 1976, p. 45): When the book came out, however, some European countries were not ready for the message. The following passage was deleted in the German edition:

The most remarkable new pattern of all is emerging right now, under our eyes: There is evidence that the aging process is different for four-dimensional women. The lifetime work of Dr. Charlotte Buehler at the University of Southern California, work begun nearly fifty years ago in Vienna, and the implications of a massive study still in progress at the University of Chicago indicate that women who use their abilities don't suffer menopause as a "little death" but as a new stage of growth. From Dr. Buehler's work, it would seem that women who pursue a conscious goal for their life, expressed in creative work, reach the height of their human powers in the last half of their life, long after the so-called bloom of physical maturity. For men and women who live by larger purposes—scientists, artists, statesmen, teachers, philosophers—the peak is not yet in sight at fifty. The new millions of women with such purposes, the four-dimensional women, seem to follow such a "human curve of life." Physically, they appear to age differently from other women.

I could see this as I went around the country seeking them out. They all looked ten or twenty years younger than they were, not in the embalmed sense of a woman who . . . tries to hide her age with make-up, but in the bloom of their eyes and skin and in the vitality that burned inside. . . . They were intensely alive women.

Friedan says, "They all looked . . . younger than they were." Turn that around: They looked as young as they actually were because forty, fifty, and sixty simply isn't old anymore. These women whom Friedan observed are the best illustration that it is what we do, not how old we are chronologically, that determines how alive we are. It's high time we began to think differently about age.

The images that the ages forty, fifty, sixty, and seventy conjure up are left over from the nineteenth century. If people had their age pasted smack in the center of their foreheads, we wouldn't think twice about those numbers. Most people are actually older than you think they are.

Let me draw on my own experiences. Last summer I spent three months living in a hotel in Italy, and I played a game with the hotel porter. I would try to guess the age of the guests as they arrived. He would then compare my estimates with the dates on their passports. I was wrong almost every time.

I was way off base in the particular case of a tall, slender, blonde woman who arrived with another woman in mid-July. She was from Munich and she was head of a nursery school. Normally she wore long skirts, but her figure was good enough to show off in a bathing suit. One day she sunned at the hotel pool instead of at the beach and was the object of many an envious glance. The hotel manager fell madly in love with her. From the fourth day on, a fresh bouquet of roses appeared on her table every day. I figured she was forty-three. She was sixty-five.

Unfortunately, not everybody can play this game, even though it would definitely soothe our fear of aging. But we can play another one: When an abstract age comes up in conversation, think of a well-known face to go with it and immediately the abstract figure will lose its threat. Start right now: If somebody mentions in a derogatory way "a woman of fifty," replace the figure fifty with the face of *Jacqueline Kennedy, Shirley MacLaine,* or *Sophia Loren.* And if you need sharper ammunition, buy *Playboy*'s November 1981 issue and admire fifty-one-year-old *Vicky LaMotta,* former wife of boxer Jake LaMotta, giving her all to the fans. (The project was proposed by the magazine after the release of *Raging Bull,* a movie about the career of LaMotta.)

Do you get the idea? You have to train yourself to beat the numerical figure and those frightening, old-fashioned associations it evokes. You have to teach yourself to react fast. If people depress you by painting a black picture of old age, ask immediately precisely which age they are talking about. If the answer is "oh, from seventy onward," then think of *President Reagan* or *Katharine Hepburn,* who is still going strong at seventy-three. If the answer is eighty, think of the charming face of the British *Queen Mother* or of the striking features of sculptress *Louise Nevelson.* If someone has the nerve to suggest that women of sixty are no longer attractive, then picture the lovely *Lena Horne* and order the guy to go and see her Broadway show.

The faster you learn this game, the better. Of course there are lots of people around who at eighty-two don't look like the Queen Mother, but this is not the point. We have been overfed with grim images of age. We have purposely been shown only the black side, and it is high time we set the pendulum swinging in the right direction again. Not everyone looks superb at eighty, but a great many people do indeed, and this is all that matters to set our minds right.

What you should do, ideally, is to find your own role models for this game—in your family, your neighborhood, or at work. But make sure the people don't lie. And, since I left out the age group hovering around forty, if that figure still frightens you, imagine the faces of *Susannah York, Ali MacGraw, Judy Collins, Mary Tyler Moore, Jane Fonda, Candice Bergen, Catherine Deneuve,* and *Gloria Steinem,* to name only a few.

When I visited Steinem in her editorial offices at *Ms.* magazine a few years ago, I was astonished to see how young she looked though I knew she had just turned forty. Steinem helps other women acknowledge the natural aging process by celebrating her birthdays openly and proclaiming her age quite publicly. The first time she did so, she told a *Newsweek* reporter why: in order to show that women stay young longer than men do. Furthermore, she said, many women look young even at advanced ages, but they don't dare admit how old they are because they feel so insecure. Says Steinem, "I want to bring the truth to the surface and help to put an end, once and for all, to the lies that younger is better."

Another fact very few people know about is that older women are quite capable of strenuous physical activity. *Martha Graham,* the founder of the modern dance—and fairy godmother to the Dance Repertory Theater of the 1930s—performed onstage until she was eighty, her grace putting many a twenty-year-old to shame. *Alicia Alonso,* founder of and prima ballerina of the National Ballet of Cuba, has danced well into her sixties. German film director *Leni Riefenstahl* learned skin diving at the age of seventy. She is now equally renowned for her underwater documentaries.

Another little-known fact: For many years nearly all the private planes sold by American firms to clients in Germany, Austria, and Yugoslavia were flown singlehandedly by an elderly American woman, *Louisa Sacchi,* who retired only recently. Though well into her seventies, she could fly a single-engine plane from Wichita, Kansas, to Munich, West Germany, in thirty-five hours. She could shorten that to twenty-five hours in a twin-engine plane, if the winds were favorable. Once, in the middle of winter, she found herself 10,000 feet over the Atlantic Ocean when the heating system failed. She saw it through, even though the outside temperature was eighteen degrees below zero.

Louisa Sacchi often flew from Wichita to Munich to London and then back to Kansas twice in one week. In the years 1976–77 she flew solo to deliver thirty-five Beechcraft Bonanza F-33A training planes to the Spanish air force. She delivered thirty planes each year to the firm of Denzel in West Germany. She also flew planes to Australia and the South Seas. Not bad for an "old" lady, don't you think!

Louisa Sacchi isn't the only older woman who loves to fly. In 1978 an eighty-year-old English woman named *Mrs. Bruce* took up flying again so she wouldn't forget her favorite sport. Mrs. Bruce had once *owned* an airline, was first in the history of flying to put stewardesses on her planes, and in 1930 flew solo around the world in a rickety biplane. She had to make seventeen emergency landings because of engine trouble, but she kept on going. At that time such a flight was a colossal undertaking for anyone, man or woman, and it took a lot of courage even to make an attempt.

More tales of "older" women and the planes they piloted: *Jacqueline Auriol,* Frenchwoman, housewife, and mother, decided out of the blue that she wanted to become a test pilot. Though in 1949 she barely escaped with her life from a crash, she did not give up flying but instead flew every type of test jet, including the ill-fated Mirage III fighter, breaking velocity records right and left.

Her closest rival was another Jacqueline, *Jacqueline Cochran,* who became the first woman to break the sound barrier. That was in 1954. At the age of fifty-three she set a world speed record in a Northrup T-38, and at the age of fifty-six she flew a German air force Starfighter at twice the speed of sound. After the war she set up a flying school in England.

Jacqueline Cochran, in contrast to Auriol, had come from a background of severe poverty. She was an orphan, and her adoptive parents were so poor they couldn't even send her to school. She went to work at the age of eight, leaving school to work in a cotton mill in order to support herself. Later, she became a maid, then a cosmetician and hairdresser.

27

She stopped flying a few years ago, but she hasn't retired. Now over seventy, she owns a citrus plantation and has adopted five orphans in order to spare them the kind of childhood she lived through.

It's not beauty, luck, youth, or chance that makes us succeed in life, but our inner strength, determination, and personality. America's first "sex symbol," *Mae West,* wrote in her autobiography, "You can sing like Flagstad, dance like Pavlova, or act like Sarah Bernhardt. [But] if you don't have personality, you'll never be a star." Obviously more than a sex goddess, Mae West was an outstanding actress and became one of the most important figures in the entertainment business.

Her autobiography, entitled *Goodness Had Nothing to Do With It,* is the best antidote for age fright I can think of. Mae West was no baby when she made her first film: She was forty. Her autobiography, published when she was sixty-six, followed a succession of witty and intelligent plays and television scripts written by this great "older" woman. Discussing the secret of her lifelong success with men, she confided, "My admirers were, for the most part, important and respected gentlemen who found me desirable because I wasn't like all the others. They quickly found out I didn't care about all the old-fashioned rules that hampered a woman's freedom. I never played the helpless thing, and I laughed over the myth that women were lost without the protection and wisdom only a man could offer. This confused them, made them angry at times, but, oddly enough, they never even dreamed of leaving me on that account. To the contrary, *I* had the greatest trouble getting rid of *them.*"

Looked at dispassionately, dread of aging is pure self-deception, nothing other than a fear of life itself. It is basically a reflection of our mental, not our physical, state.

That depression that comes over us on our bad days is the same whether it's our adolescent distress over a new pimple on our forehead or, later in life, the discovery of small wrinkles at the same spot.

I can't stress this enough: Life is not just outward appearance. Much more important are inner qualities: personality, initiative, creativity, and the glow that comes with accomplishment. If you have but one of these to your credit, you'll be much more successful in later life than in your youth—and you'll be loved and respected as well.

Finally, another positive example. In the fall of 1978 the widow of composer Igor Stravinsky made headlines throughout England. *Vera Stravinsky,* an accomplished painter, flew from New York to England to be at the opening of an exhibit of some of her works in a fashionable London gallery. A whole crew of photographers and newsmen was waiting for her at Heathrow.

As she emerged from the plane, slim and spry in her full-length mink coat, the press corps could hardly believe its eyes. They had expected a feeble old lady, not this sparkling woman of the world. Vera Stravinsky was ninety-one years old. When she was asked her secret, her answer was straightforward: "It's all very simple: I work, I travel, I never let anybody scare me, and I take great pleasure in the beautiful things in life."

2

The Right Kind
of Beauty Will Last Forever

One of the greatest shortcomings of our age is that we are too impatient. Although we live longer than ever before, we are incapable of taking our time, of waiting for the right moment, of concentrating on long-term projects. If we want something, we want it fast. We insist on instant gratification. We see something or hear of something that appeals to us, and we want it NOW, as if we had only six months left to live.

All those rules set up by modern, Western societies seem to be invented for people with only a very short lifespan. Consider, for example, the ideas that a man has to make it professionally by the age of thirty and that a girl of thirteen has to have a steady boyfriend. Now, why should they? I can only pity those who reach their peak at thirty. What can possibly please them when they are fifty or sixty? What kind of existence can we expect if we drive ourselves too fast at too young an age? What will happen to those who use up all the energy that was meant to last a lifetime by the age of thirty? I can tell you what happens. If you reach the peak at thirty, at thirty-one you will think that you are past your prime. The same goes for beauty.

Who says that a woman has to be fabulous as soon as she reaches her teens? It is much better for a woman's future development if, at age thirteen, she play with her dolls or train sets instead of her boyfriends. We all seem to have forgotten that adolescence is a time of preparation and not of fulfillment, that in our teens we should prepare our beauty so that it will last a lifetime. Have you forgotten the old saying: "Good things come to those who wait"? Well, it is still true today, especially where modern men and women are concerned. If you rush natural development, if you mature too fast, you are in trouble. You'll be burned out at an early age. Only those who ripen gradually have a chance of living a full life. Those popular theories of making it fast in every way are debatable at best. In reality, the world belongs to the late bloomer.

A young girl who is not attractive at sixteen shouldn't despair; she can be so at thirty-five. If she's beautiful at thirty-five, she'll be so at sixty and for the rest of her life, because the kind of beauty you create yourself never fades.

Some women never seem to change, even when you don't see them for five or ten years at a time. They never seem to lose their attractiveness. Not long ago, one such woman, a fifty-year-old architect, showed me a picture taken of herself years earlier. I couldn't believe it. At twenty-five she was overweight, plain, had bad skin and equally bad posture. "I wasn't able to pull myself together until I was thirty," she said, "but once I did, it stuck."

The hardest years in any woman's life are those between twenty and thirty when she loses her illusions about love and will probably marry. Suddenly, her life has boundaries and duties and often she's still unfulfilled.

Those years of stress, of the small apartment, small children, and small budgets, during which the one-time admirer has become a husband, take their toll on many women in the form of extra pounds and a few premature lines—lines that shouldn't appear on a twenty-five-year-old face, that normally first emerge on a successful, single woman's face some ten years later. It's quite a shock to discover them for the first time, to find that they linger around your eyes and mouth long after you have stopped laughing. "But I'm so young, what next?" You say in desperation, and with each birthday you get more and more frightened.

A lot of women avoid this by structuring their lives differently. They use their twenties to grow, to continue their schooling, to study, travel, work and build a career. Then, if they do want a family, they have their children in their thirties or even later, at a time when the worst financial struggle is over and their feet are firmly on the ground. More on this in chapter 5, "In Praise of Mature Motherhood."

However, if you have taken the traditional road, nothing is lost. Wrinkles are not that important and, if they really bother you, you can get rid of them later on with the help of cosmetics, facial massage, relaxation exercises, or even plastic surgery.

On the other hand, you can also learn to love those wrinkles. On some faces they look definitely great—it all depends what type of person you are. If you have a lined face and hide it in shame, you are signaling to people: Wrinkles are bad. But if you show your face with self-assurance, never shunning the light, never avoiding people's glances but looking straight into their eyes, you are fine. If you show the world that you like yourself and those wrinkles of yours, the world will like them too.

Certain German family magazines have written with great enthusiasm about Nancy Reagan's wrinkles, swearing that they enhance her face. The French, too, are entranced by Mrs. Reagan's mature beauty. They think her more attractive and elegant than the young Jacqueline Kennedy. (They also say that Jacqueline Kennedy has much more class now.)

Always remember: Whether you like your wrinkles or not, they cannot destroy your sex appeal. Your skin is not your main asset. Your character is, and your personality. So far every man with whom I've ever been intimate has had more wrinkles than I, and they never bothered me in the least. When I'm in love with somebody, I also love the lines around his eyes. They express something about his personality. Then there's my Parisian friend Tilda who, at fifty-five, naturally has a few wrinkles. Every time I see her kissed by her lover, who is nearly seventeen years younger than she, I know a smooth complexion is not all there is to life.

Most men know a good thing when they see it, and they won't let wrinkles interfere. They hardly even notice them on the face of an attractive woman and, if they do, it's only a first, fleeting impression. After the initial exchange of words, the first laugh, the sparkle in her eyes, the humor—in short, as the warmth of her personality comes through—the wrinkles are forgotten.

Women often worry needlessly about such things. Magazine and television ads feed this insecurity, so women sit at home, bored, believing they have no purpose in life and no interests; and because they have never experienced success, they blame their wrinkles for their unsatisfactory lives.

One of my friends once confided to me, "When I was thirty I thought life was over. My husband had left me, and there I was with two small children. I was desperate. Now I realize that divorce was the best thing that could have happened to me. Our marriage had become an absolute hell. If I hadn't been forced to act independently, I never would have accomplished a thing." Today she's forty-four, looks terrific, dresses fashionably, and has a job as head bookkeeper in a large company. She has bought a vacation home near Salzburg, Austria; the children are nearly grown; and, after a number of short-lived affairs, she has formed a good and enduring relationship with a man two years her junior.

What I'm trying to point out is that beauty is intimately connected with the kind of life you lead. A contented person will never become old and ugly. If you live halfway sensibly, don't abuse your body, and don't drink or smoke too much, you have nothing to fear.

Speaking of the body, even though beauty comes for the most part from inside and manifests itself through the glow of your personality, it's well known that body skin remains young longer than facial skin, mainly because it's protected by clothing. The surgeon who operated on my sixty-five-year-old Hungarian grandmother told family friends he was so surprised at her unblemished and beautiful body he could hardly bear to take his scalpel to it.

My mother, at the age of eighty-two, still has skin that is smooth and elastic, as was true of my beloved Austrian grandmother. I remember how astonished I was by her silken skin when, shortly before her death at the age of eighty-four, she asked me to rub an ointment into her aching back. Of course, I realize such physical attributes are partly genetic in nature, but surely they also relate to the fact that the women in my family have found the right balance between fat and thin and have stuck to it. Even so, it was a complete revelation to me that elderly people, contrary to all the propaganda, can have attractive bodies.

Adolescents are almost never satisfied with their figures. Remember your own agonies, standing in front of a mirror trying on your first prom dress? You found yourself too fat, too flat-chested, too skinny, too tall, or too short. Perhaps you thought, *I'm not even eighteen, and nothing's right. What will I look like when I'm older?*

The answer is, you will look better. A woman comes to terms with her body when she's grown, when she discovers that others who she believed were perfect beauties have similar complexes. She'll accept her body when she's with a man who thinks she's beautiful. On the other hand, she may have the most gorgeous body imaginable and still be miserable if she's in love with one whose idea of the perfect woman doesn't match her measurements.

A very dear friend whom I've know since childhood has what we would call a stunning figure: narrow waist, beautiful bosom, good legs . . . and what happened? She fell in love with a sculptor who never appreciated her, mainly because he basically preferred men. He once confided to me: "I've always been afraid of a big bosom." My friend, who loved this man with great tenacity from the time she was fifteen until she was thirty-two, felt she was unattractive all this time. She hunched her shoulders in order to hide her breasts, suffered agonies, and in the end, after ten years of waiting, she attributed her "failure" to being over twenty-five. It wasn't until she went abroad to pursue her career as a painter, and met and fell in love with an American sociologist who loved her just the way she was, that she began to blossom. When I saw her a few weeks ago, she looked like a different person, radiant and years younger, walking with self-assurance and showing off her beautiful bosom for the first time in her life.

I'd like to point out a parallel: Renoir was a great painter, but among those who do not appreciate the Impressionists he will receive little acclaim. All of us, whether we are painters or writers, journalists or fashion designers, male or female, have to find our own audience in life if we want to be happy. We can find it, but we have to take pains to do so.

There is no doubt that for the past thirty years, during the so-called sexual revolution, the media have helped to drill into women an exaggerated fear of aging. Among the most "successful" in this respect are magazines "for men" and the advertising industry. Both have created artificial images of beauty, with little or no foundation in reality. As a result, the uncritical reader was soon convinced that beauty is indeed only skin deep and an absolute synonym of youth. Even worse, women, confronted year after year with these pictures of plastic bodies, started to try to compete. Of course they fought a losing battle.

There is no way any mortal, man or woman, can compete with a photographic image. The attempt is always fatal. What you admire (or fear) on those glossy pages or those larger than life posters does not exist. It is an illusion created by a hard-working team of makeup artists, photographers, layout experts, and a willing woman or girl who is only interested in the money she makes on the set.

I wish you could all be present in the studio when such fashion photos or nude pictures are being taken. You would be amazed how much time and energy, how many special lighting effects, rehearsals, and makeup tricks it takes to transform an ordinary girl or woman into the "perfect" body. Photographing a woman's breasts is one of the most difficult tasks in the world. I once saw a photographer working with sticky-tape trying to glue them into shape. As I said, one day on the set and you're rid of your depression because you will have seen with your own eyes that it was only an illusion that induced such tremendous feelings of inferiority. *Nobody looks like those super-*

women in the centerfold—least of all the models them-selves.

Indeed, once you have looked behind the scenes, you breathe easier. Without makeup, these women are ordinary mortals. You would never recognize them in private life. One of my London neighbors was a model. For a long time I had admired her pictures in various English fashion magazines without realizing that this dazzling creature was Maggie from next door. On the set she wore false eyelashes, glowing wigs, and layers and layers of makeup. At home she was friendly, pale, and childlike. Her natural hair was thin and carrot-colored. She had not a hint of a bust, and nobody turned to look at her twice when she went shopping on Saturday morning dressed in jeans and a sweater, and without a trace of makeup. She had nothing whatsoever in common with her public image. Like so many other fashion models, she was not in the least interested in seducing other women's husbands. She was home-loving and absolutely faithful to her fiancé. She desperately wanted children—and has since had them to her own and her husband's satisfaction.

Maggie once gave a big party. The agency for which she worked was taking part in a Miss World contest. Maggie invited several of the contestants and a few of the top models to her apartment. For days I agonized over what to wear so I wouldn't look out of place. The big night came. I walked through the door . . . into a room full of perfectly ordinary-looking people. I was shaken. Somehow I had imagined all those girls to be of superhuman dimensions, on pedestals bathed in light, just like their photos in the slick magazines. What a relief to realize not only that it was possible to meet them face to face but to find that they weren't all that extraordinary. None of them made a real impact. Most had little to say; and the largest group of people congregated around an American singer who wasn't beautiful at all but told a good story.

What goes for models applies equally to film stars, actors, and ballet dancers. Those people who look superhuman under the stage lights sometimes are hardly recognizable when you see them later in their dressing rooms or at an after-theater party. The elfinlike dancers of the Béjart Brussels Opera ensemble, both male and female, looked perfect onstage. After their premiere at the Vienna State Opera, however, I met them up close at a reception at the Belgian embassy. Most of them were small and plain and, in addition, many had bad skin.

Going to the movies can also be an exercise in ego deflation. The women on the screen are too perfect. And yet it is all make-believe. Everything, from the carefully sculptured face to the tailor-made clothes, is calculated to hide any figure flaw. The perfect lighting abolishes unflattering shadows, and makes wrinkles invisible. Nevertheless, this *illusion* of "natural" beauty has inhibited women in the audience to such an extent that they turn their heads away in shame from their male companions as soon as the house lights come on.

There is nothing more absurd. Illusion is illusion, particularly in the movies. In the winter of 1979, the English actress Jane Birkin was in Vienna filming a movie about the life of the painter Egon Schiele. The court scene was filmed in the small village of Neulengbach, just outside Vienna. It was freezing cold. The old walk-up court building was unheated, and Birkin, who played the painter's lover, had to walk through the halls dressed only in a nearly transparent short-sleeved blouse, light shoes, and a thin skirt.

When the scene was finally completed we went to a

local inn, huddled close to the stove, and began our scheduled interview. Jane Birkin sat opposite me. She was pale, obviously had a bad cold, and gazed at me with tired, watery eyes. There were shadows around her nose and mouth and, in short, she looked anything but a radiant star. And yet, in the stills our newspaper photographer had taken, she looked marvelous. The cameras had captured only those features that were beautiful: the high cheekbones, the sensuous lips, the heavy eyebrows, the straight nose. I could scarcely believe it. The picture bore hardly any resemblance to the woman who had been sitting across from me.

Jane Birkin had an explanation. "Moviemaking," she said, "is magic." And then she told a story. At the age of seventeen she went to Rome to visit her uncle, the filmmaker Carol Reed who became world famous for *The Third Man*. She asked him if she had the raw material to become a star. Reed looked at her and said, "That depends entirely on the camera. The camera has to fall in love with you."

How, when, and why the camera becomes enamored, nobody knows. But Jane was lucky. She belonged to the chosen few. She called it "magic" that her features appeared more beautiful on celluloid than they did in person. We would say these people are photogenic, and important in this context, photogenic people are no threat.

Real beauties are hard to find. Film directors often search for years for actresses who are both photogenic and talented. And it is undeniably a talent to be able to create on command a never-never world of beauty you don't actually possess. This isn't an easy task and should be admired as an artistic achievement. It should not be regarded as a threat to people outside the film industry.

Ever since that evening at Maggie's, I have understood

what goes into the making of a so-called ravishing beauty.
And I have stopped automatically comparing myself to the
women in fashion magazines, on television, or in films. I
advise you strongly to do the same. Compare yourself to
real people, and see how you make out. Trying to compete
with an illusion always ends in disaster.

So much for general insecurity. Now to specifics—beginning with our bustlines. Note the following: A woman
who has a good bosom when she's thirty-five will have it
when she's sixty-five, provided she takes care of herself,
remains healthy, and avoids drastic fluctuations in weight.
A beautiful bust, first of all, is a question of one's genes
and not of age. A woman whose bosom droops by the time
she's in her late twenties probably never had a beautiful
bust anyway. Doctors know this and the women concerned do, too, but the latter are loath to admit it. This is
understandable. In their fantasies, at least, they would like
to have what nature denied them. You've heard them say,
"If you had seen me at seventeen, you wouldn't have believed your eyes." When a man hears this, he thinks, *Aha,
the female figure starts to get flabby after twenty.* A
woman hearing the same thing is paralyzed by fears of
getting older.

The myth that only very young women have good bustlines is, thank heavens, finally dying out. There was, however, an historical reason for this belief, valid for about
three hundred years: the corset.

From the seventeenth through the nineteenth centuries, men demanded "feminine" women with "feminine"
bodies, that is, with the emphasis on the breasts and hips.
This was achieved by lacing the waist relentlessly until it
was half its normal size. In royal families even children
were laced. In others, very young ladies were exempt from

this torture. However, from the time girls were presented to society and became marriageable, they had to submit to the corset, and—like it or not—to all of its related discomforts. People spoke openly of the symptoms: shortness of breath, liver and stomach complaints, fainting spells. And in due course women's figures went to shambles. The waist turned into an unattractive band of ribbed flesh and the bosom drooped.

Even as recently as 1905, when many European women still wore corsets, Dr. Anna Fischer Dueckelmann denounced the injurious effects of this ridiculous garment. (Anna came from a family of famous physicians and received her M.D. from the University of Zurich.) She wrote, "A slackness in the breast tissue is something that occurs in all women, young and old, slender and heavy. The deplorable cause of both the underdevelopment of the breast glands and the breast muscles is the corset." Anna Dueckelmann was, for this reason, one of the leading advocates of the so-called reform movement for the abolition of the corset and the adoption of more sensible clothing for women.

No sooner had the corset disappeared then the bosom was restored to full bloom. Most women have attractive breasts, in keeping with their figure types. But only now, more than seventy years later, is the public accepting this fact. The change in attitude can be observed in the popularity of dresses and blouses designed to be worn without a bra, no matter how old the wearer. What this indicates is that women are no longer ashamed of their bodies, that they finally have enough self-confidence to say to the world: Look at me. I'm beautiful just the way God made me.

This movement away from the dictates of the fashion designers of earlier periods and their unnatural, artificially

41

pushed-up bosom is very good news. All over the world women flock to buy designer clothes that are made for real women and not for some imaginary sex doll. Fashion today is cheerful, free/flowing, colorful, embroidered and pleated, often influenced by the national costumes of Asia and the Orient. Fabrics are softer and natural fibers are back, comfortably draping the silhouette rather than forcing it into a mold.

I have lived in Paris for a number of years and was able to observe this change at firsthand. The breakthrough came one evening at an exclusive dinner party given by the American ambassador at his residence. Some of the wealthiest women in town were present. And what did they wear? Those little dresses from the boutiques on the Boulevard St. Michel that any woman could afford. And they looked beautiful, although many of them were well advanced in years.

I remember one particular dress very well. It was a simple olive-green wool dress with long sleeves and an embroidered top. I had seen it selling for very little in the window of a small shop near the St. Michel métro station. On this particular evening, the wife of the director of the Atlantic Institute wore it. She was over fifty and looked great. And to me she was the proof that the worst was over, that women were finally realizing that cheerful, colorful, and even slightly kooky clothes aren't just for the very young. A woman of any age can wear anything she chooses as long as it suits her and she feels at ease. The time when women over forty were forced to appear in what amounted to sackcloth and ashes—the gray tailored suit—is gone for good.

A few final remarks on the theme of the bustline. Self-discipline, exercise, enough sleep, a careful diet, moderate smoking and drinking—these will keep you fit. Otherwise there are hardly any other rules. A cold shower after your bath is good for you. Too much direct sunlight is bad. Live naturally, don't overdo, and you've nothing to fear. Even pregnancy won't damage your breasts unless you follow the custom practiced in some parts of Africa where a child is suckled until the age of three. A healthy woman can cope with nursing her child for nine months with no problem, and this is much better than artificially stopping the flow of milk and risking inflammation.

I know it is easier said than done, but we have to rid ourselves, as fast as possible of all those dangerous clichés we have grown up with concerning age. Every one of us is haunted by prejudices, preconceived notions, silly stories told to us by neighbors or relatives, probably with good but misguided intentions.

When I think back to my youth, I am still dismayed at the vast number of "truisms" grownups had in store for us. But we were too inexperienced and frightened to fight back. Young as we were, we mistook opinion for bare fact.

For instance, when I was sixteen, one of my neighbors told me, "Well, you're sixteen and still slender, but when you're thirty, you'll have to decide between your figure and your face." I was flabbergasted, but I believed her. Immediately, my mind set to work. I first imagined myself as a bulky matron with a smooth complexion, then fashionably thin with a face wrinkled like a dried apple. Perhaps I should explain that in Austria (where I grew up), in the late fifties and sixties, it was very easy to tell the single girl from the married woman: The latter was usually some forty-five pounds heavier. Being fat meant you were tied down, you had no more fun in life, you were no longer young.

All of my girlfriends were terrified at the thought of putting on weight. Being thin was more desirable than being beautiful. The prospect of having to ruin your figure at the age of thirty in order to avoid getting wrinkles was like a death sentence.

Of course, a woman doesn't have to make such decisions at thirty, forty, fifty, or sixty. Nothing changes overnight, yet somebody is always warning us, "Just wait until you're forty," and all sorts of horrible images come to mind.

Cosmetic firms and advertising agencies take advantage of these fears. They package and promote products for the "woman over thirty" or the "career woman over fifty," with the result that we are convinced we'll lose our attractiveness from one day to the next, that between the years twenty-nine and thirty, and then again between forty-nine and fifty, lies a fathomless pit into which we will inexorably stumble. Of course, this is nonsense. Nothing changes from one birthday to the next.

"I had been warned that there was some major rite of passage involved in turning forty," actress *Susan Strasberg* told *Harper's Bazaar* reporters, "but I was so busy writing [her hit memoir *Bittersweet*] that I didn't even notice it. There's supposedly a standard way to feel at every age and I think that's nonsense."

And, of course, she is right. You feel the same as always, whatever age you are. The changes are very slight and they are mostly on the surface. The human body does not suddenly stop developing. There is always time for improvement, whether you are in your forties or fifties, and even at sixty and seventy you can enhance your figure and posture through exercise. Our bodies are not static. As long as we breathe, there is hope.

There is a simple rule to being beautiful. If you want to charm others, you have to learn how to like yourself. If a woman believes she is neither attractive nor desirable, nobody else will see those qualities in her. If she does not respect herself, men won't respect her either. If she is not happy with herself, she will come across as a negative person, she'll be full of inhibitions in bed, and her lovers won't come back.

Now, getting to like oneself is easier at present than ever before. All you have to do is to accept your own individual kind of beauty. Once you have done that, you are all right. Times have changed. The natural attraction between the sexes has proved stronger than any short-lived preferences for small and plump or tall and slender women. There is far less categorizing as "feminine" or "unfeminine." You are what you are. Individual beauty is here to stay. Don't try to emulate a certain "type" of woman because it is suddenly chic to look like Marilyn Monroe or Isadora Duncan. It rarely works. Analyze what you yourself have got and use your energies to make the best of your particular assets. Furthermore, what some men consider beautiful has never ceased to amaze me.

Case in point: I know an art dealer of Canadian-Austrian origin who, at the age of twenty-four, fell in love with a black woman ten years older than he was, and the mother of four children. Louisa had been deserted by her husband and was collecting welfare. For days on end this man raved about her. He described in glowing details their marvelous mornings in bed together, praising her passionate responses until I was green with envy. When I finally asked him what she looked like, his answer so amazed me that I have remembered it to this day, word for word: "She has a potbelly and her breasts hang very low. But I don't mind and neither does she. She is fabulous. She has the most beautiful back I've ever seen."

Doesn't that tell us something about individual beauty?

This fabulous Louisa could not be called beautiful by usual standards. And yet this man raved about her seductive back. It was marvelous. And I learned my lesson: Even if you have but one good feature to your credit, you can be loved because of it.

I learned even more about this in France. I have lived in Paris on and off for seven years now and, believe me, it is a great place for social studies. French women are certainly not more beautiful than English, German, Swedish, Italian, or American women. But the French woman is one step ahead of us all in that she has perfected the art of selling herself. She is so adept at calling attention to her excellent features, you'll never notice she also has some less attractive ones. If she is ugly as sin and yet is endowed with a swanlike neck, it is this neck that will haunt your sleep.

Some time ago, the well-known French film director Claude Chabrol came to Austria to shoot the last sequence of a TV series. Among his entourage were Helmut Berger, Chabrol's usual camera team, and Aurore Josquiss, the script girl.

Josquiss is all right. Ageless and awe-inspiring on her job, attractive but not breathtaking, she is known to protect Chabrol from strangers and journalists with the same vehemence a dog guards his bone. Chabrol had promised me an interview, and I duly appeared on location. Aurore received me with a black look.

They were filming in an old, dusty Viennese mansion on the Ring, a famous boulevard encircling the inner city. There was the usual chaos of lighting equipment, heaps of black cable, and tracks for the camera. Aurore Josquiss was all business. Instead of taking care of me and helping me find Chabrol, she sat on the ground and scribbled on her writing pad. She was dressed in nondescript corduroy pants and a beige pullover. Her blond hair was piled non-chalantly on top of her head. She was in a bad mood and it didn't increase her charm.

However, she would not have been French if she hadn't done the inevitable, namely, draw attention to herself and her best features. She was squatting on the ground, all right, but in such a way that your eyes were immediately drawn to her dainty little feet. These feet were enclosed in the most beautiful leather boots imaginable, polished to a perfect sheen, the kind you would only buy once every five years and most certainly not wear on dusty locations. Yet there they were. And whatever Josquiss did—sit on the ground, step into the light, or over ladders, hop over boxes, recline on a sofa and cross her legs—she did it with such proficiency that those tiny feet remained the center of attention.

I was not the only one who noticed them. When I talked about her to our photographer after the interview was finished, he said: "Sorry, I was not listening closely—who are you talking about? The girl with the pretty feet?"

That's know-how!

Women are too timid. For generations they have let themselves be frightened by traditional nonsense. Yet the world has changed. What was valid once does not apply today. Clothes no longer make the man. Tall women are indeed finding husbands, and baby-fine hair is not the end of the world. The controversy over fine hair is, in fact, a perfect example of the ease with which we women allow ourselves to be talked into inferiority complexes.

For years there was a campaign to "combat" fine hair. Having fine hair, in the experts' opinion, was second only to having the plague. The verdict: Keep it short and keep it permanented. Practically every hairdresser offered the same advice—and why? Because, as I found out by asking some of them, thick hair is easier to manage and to work into elaborate hairdos. The reason for the whole uproar, and one that caused many women a lot of misery, interestingly enough was expediency!

Talking about hair, there's no reason for anyone to be ashamed of having soft, silky, fine hair. It is nicer to touch and, if you want to wear it long, do so by all means and be happy. One thing we must stop doing is confusing the experts' opinion with the word of God. I am constantly amazed how slavishly women adhere to "professional" advice, swallowing uncritically what their doctors, hairdressers, beauticians, and dressmakers tell them. Every stranger gets a chance to make us miserable. Salespeople in dress shops or drugstores can convince us within seconds that our physical appearance is so flawed that only some very costly remedy will help. Cosmetic counters, in particular, are breeding grounds for complexes. And the latest sales techniques make sure that they will remain so.

If, for example, you are looking for shampoo, the sales clerk no longer asks, "What kind would you like?" No, she puts on a frown, directs a very concerned glance directly at your hair, and asks, "What kind of problem do you have?" If you dare answer that you're not aware of any but nevertheless would prefer to go about with clean hair, she gets very annoyed. As far as she is concerned, *everybody* has a hair problem. And beware! Her all-knowing smile and skeptical look will convince you that, of course, she is right. That you do need special treatment, that your hair is either as dry as straw, or drab, dull, fly-away, oily . . . in short, that it is wrong from beginning to end.

What we all should do is say the following: "Are you trying to insult me? I'd simply like a good shampoo, and if you persist in finding fault with me I'll never set foot in this store again." If you say this in a loud and determined voice, preferably within earshot of the store manager (who will begin to understand that this technique does not go down well) the salesclerks will soon be asking in friendly tones again: "May I help you?"

Women still have to learn to stand up for themselves. If somebody confidently tells a woman that her hands are really unattractive and her look not what it should be, her first reaction is to believe it. This has to change. We have to learn to be content with ourselves. We are the way we are, and others will have to like it or lump it.

The road to success is obvious. Don't complain about what you don't have (or allude to it in company) but concentrate on what you have and learn to display it to your advantage, whether it's a good back, hands, hair, or neck. A woman who believes she has no physical charms need only think of the impression a beautiful voice, graceful movement, well-modulated speech, and unique way of expressing oneself can make. There simply is no such thing as a woman who is not beautiful in some way or other.

Let us turn now to the complexion and, dread of dreads, wrinkles. Not everybody gets them. There are always exceptions: those women who look perpetually young, women of fifty who have retained a smooth complexion without resorting to a face-lift. I know a woman like that. She happens to be an American actress who is fifty-one years old and hasn't a line on her face. She divulged her secret: "Never frown, don't laugh too often, and rub Vaseline around your eyes every night." She added, "One thing is certain. The day I find a wrinkle on my face, I'll have a heart attack." In answer to my question about whether she would really feel insecure if she found laugh lines on her face at sixty, she answered, "Of course. I don't want to show the world that I've lived."

In my opinion, this is a mistake. The world is impersonal enough as it is. Do we have to make it even more so with characterless faces? I'm personally fascinated by lines and furrows in a person's face. These give clues to the life he or she lives and has lived. Overall, I find older faces much more interesting than younger ones, and nearly every artist will agree with me. Don't forget, as long as you're not set in your ways, your face won't become set like a mummy's either. Remember this, and growing older will only bring physical and mental advantages.

Naturally, it takes time to change one's thinking. I too, wasted precious time in my youth worrying about getting wrinkles. At the age of twenty-five I was newly married and living in London. I used to wander around Regent Street for hours, looking for wrinkles on the faces of the crowd around me. "What a pretty woman," I'd say to myself, "but she already has lines around her eyes. I hope she's a lot older than I am." I carried on these studies mostly during my lunch breaks, as I had a job near Piccadilly Circus. And I came up with some surprising results. I discovered that some people who had wrinkles still looked young, while others who had none looked old. Those who seemed the oldest, though they certainly couldn't have been, walked with expressionless faces, their eyes downcast. Now I know where this look comes from: It is the visible sign of resignation, beauty's worst enemy. The person who becomes resigned becomes old.

Resignation is nothing more than locking the door to all those tremendous energies that slumber in our bodies. Everyone knows the meaning of the "will to live." Every doctor knows its importance in critical life and death situations, after terrible accidents or major operations. Every doctor has said at one time or another, "Only his will to live can pull him through." When it is there, it works miracles.

The will to be young works in the same way. In both cases we simply have to give the energy that sleeps within us the chance to awaken. The person who gives in to resignation leaves these vast, often unsuspected reserves of strength untapped. She has lost more than she realizes and will be old long before her time.

The surest way to lose your youth and attractiveness is to be stuck in an unhappy or indifferent relationship. It doesn't matter whether it's a marriage or a living arrangement, whether you've been with your partner for a long or a short time. A woman who no longer receives praise, admiration, and love, who feels no longer sexually desirable, will become resigned and old.

Marriages that go sour from the start, whether because of physical or mental incompatibility—and there are large numbers of such marriages—should be dissolved as soon as possible, preferably before there are any children. The puritanical doctrine of "sticking it out" is, as far as I am concerned, a fatal mistake. You can stick it out on the job, if you have to. But even there it is a poor solution. You do much better work in a place where you like your work, your colleagues, and the higher-ups. Still, if you can't find a better job, you have to try and make the best of what you've got. But to apply those tactics to a marriage is fatal.

Love can't be forced. It is either there or it isn't. Patience cannot spark off physical desire. Either the chemistry is right or it never will be. Of course, you can work at the relationship, but the most you'll be rewarded with is a kind of polite, civilized togetherness, maybe even friendship. But friendship is not enough to keep you young and attractive. I know this from experience: Living alone is more beneficial to your looks, not to mention your psyche, than putting up for years and years with a man you don't really desire (or who doesn't desire you anymore).

As we all know, breaking up is no easy task. One needs an awful lot of energy to separate from a man one has grown accustomed to. On top of it all, your partner will not want to let you go and will start behaving like a child: He has a toy he has not looked at for a long time, does not even know whether he really likes it or not, but he is not going to let anybody take it away from him. Men do not like to be left. Neither do women. But women hate to fight losing battles, and if they realize that love is dead they let the man go. At least many younger women react that way, especially if there are no children or money considerations involved. Men, however, like to hang on. Even if there is no hope, they develop an uncanny tenacity to try and make you stay.

If these men are not physically abusive, they are sometimes mentally destructive, trying to convince the woman that she will be doomed to poverty, loneliness, and failure if she leaves the marriage. Many women let themselves be intimidated into staying. But if they do, they will soon grow very depressed and in the end give in to some disease or other, which isn't the way to stay young and lovely. If you decide not to leave, the rewards will be small. At best you'll be treated with more consideration for a few weeks, be taken on a trip—but then it's back to square one again.

I'm speaking, as I say, from experience. If your partner has neglected you for several years, if you know that he fancies somebody else, there is no hope for staying beautiful. If you like to play games, you can *act* as if you were

about to leave him, you can keep him in continuous sus-
pense to win back his interest. But this, I assure you, is
very tiring and not to everybody's liking. It means having
to lie, to play-act, to pretend. You can't be your natural
self anymore. Aside from the fact that an intelligent man
will soon see through it all, it is degrading and it doesn't
lead to your goal, which is to be loved.

If a relationship makes you unhappy, there is nothing
to do but leave. Once you have made up your mind, go
through with it fast. You have to be prepared for some
hardship, for a lot of doubts and some moments when all
you want to do is go back to him. But you will also realize
that being alone after many bad years of marriage is a
relief. Through my work as a journalist, I have met
hundreds of women who started out bravely on their own
after fifteen, eighteen, twenty years of marriage. And every
day I read their success stories in the papers. Paige Rense,
for example, was a housewife and mother until the age of
thirty-eight. After her divorce, she became one of the most
successful women in publishing. She is now, at forty-eight,
editor in chief of *Architectural Digest* and has increased
its circulation from fifty thousand to half a million. (Under
her guidance, the food magazine *Bon Appétit* went up
from a quarter of a million subscribers to one and a half
million.) Her salary is in six figures, and she is anything
but lonely. Lots of women are afraid they won't find work
after so many years in the home; if they really want, however, they always do. But back to our discussion of love.

The moment you tear yourself away from the sterile
"married-couple social life" that has involved the same circle of couples for years and years, you will discover that
there is an unbelievably large number of unattached men
around who are looking for partners. There are widowers,

bachelors, men who have gone or are going through divorce—and for the first time in years you can choose new friends.

The first twelve months or so, many women are not capable of forming lasting friendships. Often it takes two years before you want a man to stay in your life. But the relationships you do enter into can be satisfying, at least on the physical level. The new lover whom you invite home doesn't accept out of habit but because he wants to. For a woman, to be desired, to be noticed after a long unhappy relationship, is unbelievably gratifying. You'll soon notice, now that you're single, that doors are opening. You're ready again for whatever heaven provides, and heaven will provide *if* you cooperate. You simply have to be ready to meet it—and men—halfway.

This means you can't allow yourself to sit home and feel sorry for yourself. Neither should you indiscriminately bring strange men home to bed. Make the time and commitment necessary to look for an interesting career. Better your education. Or do both. Dedicate yourself completely to whatever you've decided to do. Take an interest in other people, a *genuine* interest, and thus become a more open person.

This may mean leaving a sterile suburb and moving into a city where you can find stimulation and, above all, where you'll meet people in similar situations. Many women are afraid to have dinner in a restaurant, go to a movie, see a play, or attend a reception by themselves. Don't they realize there's hardly anything more provocative than a woman coming through a door alone? Right away every man in that room is alerted to her presence. I've often been annoyed myself when a man with whom I'm seated in a restaurant begins to wonder: *Now who can that be, such an interesting-looking person? Why is she out by herself? Do you suppose I could talk to her?* All of this takes place while the solo diner feels she's an undesirable outsider among all these couples. The greatest stumbling block to making a new start is realizing and capitalizing on the opportunities your new freedom offers you.

The mirror is a great helper in setting us free from unhappy relationships. It has helped me many times. If I want to know how I'm really doing, how my spirits are, I look into the mirror, usually the one I carry in my purse. And when I do, I say either, "If I can still smile, it can't be all that bad," or, "The misery is beginning to show. It's time to take action." Then I can suddenly deal with any problem out of pure self-preservation.

The last time this happened was six years ago in Paris. I had just separated from a man to whom I had been completely faithful and devoted for five years. It was terribly difficult, but I had no choice. I felt it instinctively: Another year with that man and I would fall ill, never to recover. Even so, I was lucky. The desperation, the sleepless nights when he didn't come home at all, the insecurity about the future, the lovelessness and constant fighting showed up only marginally in my face. But I had other complaints.

My depression always started at four in the afternoon on the dot. For days my joints ached; my knees and hips hurt so much that going up the stairs became absolute agony. On the way to the Bibliothèque Nationale, getting out of the métro, inching along every step of the way through the long white corridors, the pain was excruciating. When I went up stairs, I sometimes had to hold on to the railing with both hands. It was particularly bad in winter when I wore a heavy coat. I couldn't bend down and was nearly hysterical every time I dropped anything on

the street, because it would take three or four tries before
I could grasp the key, or whatever else it was, safely in
my fingers.

When I looked at myself in the mirror, the face of a
defeated woman stared back at me. I no longer thought
myself attractive. My eyes had lost their shine, and I burst
into tears over any trivial matter. I finally projected my
own desperation onto the whole world. I remember precisely: On weekends when he had no time for me, I walked
through the streets of Paris alone, looking at the many
lighted windows and imagining that behind each one of
them an unhappy woman waited for her husband. My
whole life seemed cheerless and meaningless, and yet I
was only thirty-four.

Half a year after we parted, these symptoms were gone.
I had since returned to Austria. Four o'clock came, and I
was still in a good mood. I could listen to romantic music.
I could play the piano again without breaking into sobs at
the first note. I was even able to listen to the eleven o'clock
news on the radio. In Austria, there is a program called
"Music to Dream By" that starts just after the news. I used
to burst into tears at the first bars of the theme song. For
me, music to dream by had become music to cry by. I
hated the program and I turned it off before I would hear
the opening notes. Then one night I forgot. The first notes
of "Last Date" sounded, and nothing happened. My heart
didn't turn to stone, and life went on. At that point I knew
I had gotten over the worst.

Something else happened. The deep line on my forehead disappeared. I had always had a smooth forehead,
perhaps because when I was seven years old one of my
friends' mothers put her hand on my head and said, "Don't
frown—you'll regret it later." In any case, when I was still
in Paris, and after countless days of fighting and an end-

less night of crying into my pillow, I found a thin line had sprouted over the bridge of my nose. It began at the tip of my left eyebrow and stretched up my forehead for about half an inch. I was aghast. I blamed it on everything but my desperate mental state. I even thought I had become nearsighted and started wearing glasses; a year later, contact lenses. But the wrinkle didn't go away.

When I left Paris, I had more pressing problems to worry about. I had to survive, and, despite my friend's prophecy that I would starve to death without his support, I finished my studies on time, had some of my writing published, and finally landed a job with the best Austrian newspaper. As I said, I really didn't have time to stand in front of the mirror looking for wrinkles.

About a year later I went on vacation and for the first time in months had some leisure time. What did I discover? The wrinkle between my eyebrows had disappeared. At first I couldn't believe it, and turned this way and that so the light would fall on my face at different angles, allowing me to see even the tiniest imperfections. But my search was in vain. The exact spot where that unmistakable line had clearly stretched upward was now perfectly smooth, and is so today.

What does this prove? Only that wrinkles come and go, that they are affected by our mental state, and that we can get rid of them even once we're over thirty. Although our emotions can take their toll on our faces, the damage can be erased if we're willing to risk changing a life that has become unbearable.

Wrinkles are nothing more than tensed muscles. Our minds can control our bodies, and Indian yogis have demonstrated to what degree this is possible. A number of doctors and therapists have developed theories about so-called inner beauty care. Among them was Anna Seidel, an Austrian beautician. She called her teachings "Ismakogie." By doing certain easy exercises and relying on our own will-power, we can learn to tense or relax every muscle in our body; a few minutes a day suffice. As soon as we have mastered this control, it takes only a thought impulse to smooth a furrowed brow or prevent the corners of the mouth from sagging. Even deeply etched wrinkles can be conquered in time. The secret is to have the determination to mobilize your body's energy and to continue trying until you are able to control even the smallest muscle in your face. Even defective vision can sometimes be corrected through self-control. Determination is necessary for success. We all know people who suddenly looked ten to fifteen years younger after they changed their life-styles for the better. They overcame their fears and became more self-confident, more self-assured, and this new poise exudes from every pore.

It is certainly no accident that in many languages the most common adjective used to describe beauty is "radiant." What does this mean exactly? To radiate means to emit something positive, as the sun radiates warmth. Those impulses we send out, this animation from within is perceived in the eye of the beholder as "beauty." If a woman is filled with despair or hate, there is no way she can glow. Instead, she projects bad "vibes," as they say, and these can obscure even the greatest beauty. Sensitive people feel another's glow just as clearly as they see the physical results. If you want to stay young and beautiful, the glow has to be natural. Cosmetics won't help; the lack of inner radiance will betray you.

Beauty comes from within, from inner satisfaction. Nothing becomes a woman more than having a job that satisfies her or a lover who does the same. Let me give you an example. From time to time we all undergo changes in appearance. We know this and notice it in those around us. We all have days when we look fantastic and others when we think we look, well . . . . acceptable. This was never so clear to me as on the day after I had spent my first night back in Austria with a man who meant something to me.

It was after a summer party in the vineyards just north of Vienna. It was late in the evening, the party was almost over, and suddenly we found ourselves sitting next to one another in a small, whitewashed wine cellar. We couldn't stop talking. Without wasting words, it was clear to both of us we would spend the night together, and so we did. We didn't sleep a wink, and I was gloriously happy for the first time since I had left Paris.

The next day I returned to Vienna at about noon. I took a bath and stood in front of the mirror as if my feet had suddenly taken root. Normally the day following a sleepless night is a disaster. I usually have a headache, can hardly keep my eyes open, and can't stand myself. This time I had only one thought: *I feel and look terrific!* Of course I knew the old saying, "A good lover is the best beauty prescription," but I had never experienced it before myself.

The intensity of the need for physical love varies. There are some women who prefer to live alone and others who long for a man perhaps once a week. There are no norms. Every woman has to come to terms with her own personal desires. Physical love is a natural need and is preceded in importance only by eating and drinking. Love is a necessity of life, and a woman who doesn't have enough of it becomes bitter, envious, hard, old, and ugly. After a memorable night with a considerate man, both body and soul are at peace. This shines from our eyes and glows from our skin. It is called by one and all "beauty."

A similar feeling of fulfillment can come from satisfying mental activity. I get almost the same sensation of inner glow, of the gratification I call "beauty," when I have accomplished something in my work, when I have written a particularly important article or finished a chapter in a book, and am satisfied that I haven't wasted my day. The ideal, of course, is a mixture of both. No woman could ask for anything more than satisfaction in love and in her profession.

The world has, thank God, changed for the better. More precisely, women have won many battles in their fight for a world that is more just. We no longer have to decide between love and career. We can have both. We also know that a pretty face no longer guarantees (and never did, in fact) a happy marriage. Not long ago it was still common to hear parents say, "Our daughter is beautiful. Why should she push herself and why should we spend good money to educate her? She'll be married soon enough." Basing an entire life's happiness on good looks is more than a risky business. Beauty alone won't get you very far at all today. If there's nothing in that pretty head—be it brains, a kind nature, or a sharp wit—you'll lose on all counts: with men, with your children, and in your career. There is one thing I don't like about most modern magazines for teenage girls. The emphasis on clothes and makeup. What does a person derive from being "correctly" dressed and made up to go to a lecture if the lecture goes over her lovely head? What sort of pleasure can she get from being beautifully attired but mixing with people whose conversation is too much for her to grasp? Where's the thrill in going out with a man you bore to tears?

We are no longer living in the nineteenth century, when appearances were everything and the admonition to "look pretty and don't say a word" was rigorously followed. Then, a woman simply dared not show that she also had a mind; in society, only men did the talking. There were no universities that admitted women. It wasn't until the middle of the nineteenth century that a college for women was founded in England. The learned women of the Renaissance had been forgotten. Women were taught that their prime role in life was to be their husband's admiring and obedient companion.

This also meant they didn't open their mouths when their "lord and master" spoke. Parents of a daughter were terrified the girl might get herself a little education in the paternal library or find a way to participate in the classes the household tutor gave her brother. Girls had to promise their parents, both verbally and on paper, to hide their knowledge in the company of men.

An amusing example from eighteenth-century America shows what many people in the New World once thought of education for women. The story concerns the job application of an English tutor who had made the torturous crossing to the onetime colony. His letter was as follows:

Honored Sir,

I allow myself, sir, to offer myself as tutor to your gracious daughter. Within three months I will be able to teach her to write all the letters of the alphabet, to read all that is written, and to gain a command of algebra. If the honorable gentleman also wishes that the demoiselle learn composition, I will undertake that as well, given two months' additional time.

I would also like to assure you, honorable sir, that knowledge of reading and writing will in no way prove a hindrance to the young lady's marriageability. If you would care to inquire about this of my previous employer, Allan Brookstide in Philadelphia, you will be informed that, within six months of completing her studies, the elder demoiselle . . . was able to enter the bonds of matrimony with an upright citizen of America.

What made the men so afraid of educated women? The fact, I would venture, that they really had no great thirst for knowledge themselves and didn't want their wives showing them up. They felt much more at ease in the company of women who, for the most part, were purely decorative and concentrated on their appearance. Women had to learn to use the wiles they were permitted. They soon developed the art of communicating with a glance and a batting of their eyelashes. But their imagination was turned toward their wardrobes, toward coats, capes, lace, frills, flounces, ruffles, and other ornaments. Clothes were their only means of expression. When a woman is robbed of her speech, selecting the right color ribbon for her dress becomes a serious concern. Women also spent endless time on their hair. They sat in front of the mirror for hours before a big ball and then hardly dared move their heads for fear of disturbing their artistic coiffures.

A woman wanted to be as beautiful as possible because this was the only way she could get ahead. The poor creature had little to add to an evening's conversation and, even if she did, she didn't dare to express it. This period was no heyday for the female sex. A married woman was expected to consent to everything her husband decided, while he in turn—small wonder—was often bored at home and found his diversion in the company of courtesans.

Is it surprising that most women who felt they had something of substance to offer either never married or eventually left their husbands? Think of Florence Nightingale, the founder of the nursing profession; or of the writer George Sand. Neither of them would have been able to achieve anything had they remained housewives. Today things have changed. Beauty is not that important anymore and love and career can be compatibly integrated, if you try hard enough.

In this day and age, feeling deprived because you're not a beauty in the conventional sense is ridiculous. But if we want to be treated as equals with men, we have to learn to fight for ourselves, just as the men do. If you consider yourself neither beautiful nor attractive, if you have trouble finding a husband, then you have to pull yourself together just that much more and do what the men do: make the effort and pamper your mind. Stop watching television all day. Get out and get some qualifications. Go back to those university courses you abandoned. Teach yourself how to concentrate. Find something that really interests you and study it inside out. Try to make a career out of it.

If you think you are not beautiful, that you don't have enough womanly qualities to attract men by the droves, then you will have to boost your charms with professional knowledge, a good job, and a flattering life-style. Believe me, you are not hurting yourself by doing it. Men like a pretty face, but they are more durably impressed by a repleted bank account. They might turn their heads for a lovely figure (if you are not looking), but think at great length about Georgina's beautiful house in the country and Betty's sleek new car.

Going out and achieving something on a professional level makes you more interesting to the other sex, to your women friends, and, of course, to yourself. And don't forget: Have some pictures taken before you set out and again a few years later, after you have succeeded. You'll be surprised at your new self. And those men who were so slow to show up—well, you won't have to worry about them any more.

Many women who have found rewarding careers are so wrapped up in them that they decide it is their work that satisfies them most in life. They could have married had

63

they wanted to, but they didn't. And it was their own free choice.

Because of this, people have in the past jumped to the conclusion that successful women are unlucky in love. This, of course, is nonsense. Through my career, I have met any number of prominent women who talked to me about their private lives. If they were single, they had no shortage of lovers. Some of them were happily living with their men, some only spent weekends with them. But none of them was alone. These women told me that they were happy, and I believed them; you can tell from a woman's face whether she is or not. After several years in journalism, you get a feel for people. You sense either that their happiness is only a front or that there is genuine contentment, openness, generosity, warmth. Compared with housewives and mothers, these women seemed certainly to have chosen the better end.

Many men are proud if their wives are successful in a profession. Others prefer to have their women in the home, looking after their personal needs like full-time domestics (and they treat them accordingly). How these wives can stand it is beyond me. The love (if there is any) won't be able to make up for the drab routine of cleaning, waiting for the husband to come through the door, waiting for a little bit of recognition, waiting for something to happen, waiting for life to begin.

I hated housework when I was married. I did it for one year and shall never do it again. I don't mind cleaning up after myself. I love my apartment in Paris and like it to be tidy. If I have time, I clean everything myself, except for the windows. Sometimes I cook for friends. But never again do I want to feel responsible for a man's dirty laundry. I think it's degrading. Obviously, a lot of young married women feel the same. After the first euphoria over a remodeled kitchen or an expensive new piece of furniture has passed, the boredom sets in. Even the most carefully made-up face can't make a woman who is sick and tired of doing housework attractive; she may get on her own nerves as much as on others' and her beauty is endangered. On the other hand, a woman who goes out into the world has more to bring to her homelife, enriching it with her new experiences, insights, and accomplishments. And she will start to bloom. Success, even the smallest glimmer of it, is among the world's best beauty aids.

An interesting woman will always steal the show from a woman who is only beautiful. That certain something in her eye, her openness, understanding, education, and self-assurance will always be more than a match for a pretty face. Personality will always win out over appearance. Only at the beginning of a relationship are appearances important. After a while it's the *person* we react to, and we don't even "see" physical imperfections. On the contrary, intellectual laziness, character faults, an inability to learn—these will certainly undermine even the most ardent initial attraction.

A few more words about age: We women can learn from men. They have taken out an insurance policy against old age, the major clause of which reads: A man isn't interesting until he's gray at the temples. There's nothing wrong with this, except that it leaves out the woman; she too can benefit from her gray hair.

It's amazing to me how many women are not coloring their hair today. The result is marvelous. A youthful face ringed with silver hair does not make a woman look older but radiates an individual freshness that casts its own spell. If any of you feels that gray hair is inhibiting and finds comfort in coloring her hair, be my guest. But remember, gray hair is not synonymous with the end of youthfulness.

The same can be said of your complexion. Men have paved the way for us in this area as well. For years we have heard that a man's face isn't really formed until he is at least thirty. The same holds true for women. The English writer Mary Wollstonecraft, who was a tireless worker for equal rights, determined back at the end of the eighteenth century that a woman's face doesn't begin to be interesting until she's over thirty. At twenty, she said, a woman's countenance is still the product of nature. At thirty, it's what she has made of it; and what she has gained through experience she'll never lose.

A mature face that is neither bitter nor hard is a joy to see. There is so much to it, it conveys so much about the woman herself. It is beautiful in a way that defies competitive vanity.

A few words about time. To have time is good. To have too much time is deadly. If you have the feeling that life is passing you by, that time evaporates before you can do anything with it, you'll be helplessly trapped into appearances. There you'll stand, in front of the mirror, looking anxiously for new lines on your face and seeing the beginning of the end in every new gray hair.

Some men deserve more credit than we are generally willing to give them. (This excludes fashion designers and certain "artists" who are concerned only with form and too often see things only at superficial levels.) Women often don't see other women's faces. They see the lines. Men, on the other hand, can be more generous. I'll give you an example.

I was newly married and living in London. My husband and I were having breakfast. Suddenly he showed me a picture in the *Times* of the elderly Lady Spencer Churchill and said, "What a beautiful woman. This is an incredible face." I was too inexperienced to grasp the significance of this remark. My sense of rivalry was roused, and I responded, "But she's ancient and wrinkled." My husband, who was all of twenty-four, was indignant. "What?" he said. "Wrinkled? You don't know what you're talking about. Look at that expression. This woman has class. Nobody in his right mind notices wrinkles on such a face."

Times have indeed improved. Women's dread of wrinkles, a dread all too prevalent in the past three decades, is beginning to die out. Proof of this is everywhere; you only need to keep your eyes open. You see this particularly clearly in advertising. Ten years ago advertisers photographed only those faces untouched by experience. Five years ago, every laugh line was retouched out of the picture. For the past two years, however, real people have begun to stare down at us from the billboards. I first realized this when I noticed a new series of ads for British Airways. It showed a beaming stewardess whose tiny lines around her eyes and mouth were realistically photographed—visible proof that the youth cult is coming to an end.

3

Sexuality–
Young Lovers and
Women in Their Prime

Although the four years I spent in England were not the best years of my life, I do remember fondly the summer when I turned twenty-seven. I lived with a man who loved me very much—in London, South Kensington to be precise—in a white house with pillars in front and a hammock in the back. Our relationship was intense and honest in every way but one: I never told him I was two years older than he was. I hid my passport in a different drawer every week so he wouldn't find out the truth. At the time, I didn't quite understand the absurdity of it all.

Now, of course, I do. Here I was, twenty-seven years young, attractive, shamelessly worshiped by the man I loved, and in spite of this, what I *was* was less clear to me than what I thought I *had to be*—and that was "younger than my partner." Every time I flew home, Anthony—that was my friend's name—took me to the airport. Every time I filled out one of those white cards for foreigners leaving the country, I gave a false birth date because he was sitting next to me, watching. The official always changed the date later as I went through passport control, without saying a word.

Since then I have told Anthony all about it. He couldn't understand how two years' difference in age could have upset me so much. He laughed and started to tease me. Indirectly, this gave me the needed push toward self-knowledge. It was thanks to him that I learned of the attraction older women have on younger men. He helped me understand that a woman can be physically desirable even when she's a grandmother.

The real impulse to my changed thinking came at a party his parents gave. The guests were his father's friends: lawyers and doctors, all about the same age, from sixty on. All were well groomed, intellectual, pleasant people. Even though the party took place thirteen years ago, I remember the following scene in detail: I was sitting on a sofa in the drawing room, admiring the magnificent Persian rug at my feet, as I noticed Anthony, motionless, staring at a woman seated diagonally across from me. She was dressed in a light blue suit; she had black eyebrows, gray hair, and an open, attractive face.

Anthony kept on staring, and I remember that I began to do a slow burn. It hadn't been long since I had left my husband on Anthony's account, and here I sat, neglected, while he flirted with another woman. Finally I couldn't stand it any longer.

"What is it that fascinates you about that woman?" I asked indignantly.

He shrugged his shoulders, which hurt me all the more.

"First of all, she's not beautiful, and, secondly, she's at least as old as your father."

I'll never forget his reaction. "She is sixty-five," he said, "and I was very much in love with her before I met you. But you don't understand that. There is something about this woman." He thought for a moment and described her with a personal note of praise he very seldom used. He put on his expert's look and pronounced: "This woman is a knockout."

I could have strangled him. It wasn't until some years later, when my jealousy had long passed, that I began to realize the meaning of this incident. I began to ask myself, *Why are women afraid of getting older if a sixty-five-year-old woman still has a chance to make it with a twenty-five-year-old man? Something isn't right.* But then I forgot about it again.

The second such incident to get me thinking on the right track took place in Paris. I was then living with an American man twelve years my senior. He was professionally very successful but otherwise insecure, neurotic, and quite difficult. I was just winding up my studies, writing my dissertation, and was just about to score my first journalistic success.

Even though I was completely faithful to my friend both physically and in spirit, he simply couldn't believe that a woman so "significantly younger," as he used to put it, could be serious about him. He was uncontrollably jealous of everything and everybody: of letters from home; of telephone calls; of our custodian's cat, which sometimes came to visit me; and of course of everything in pants, near and far, particularly when the man in question was younger than he. He was convinced I was going to leave him as soon as I had finished my studies, and in order to prevent this he tried to discredit me whenever he could. "You can thank God you've got me," he would say, "and that I earn enough for the two of us. You're over thirty now, and by the time you're forty nobody will want you anyway. Men don't like women over forty." In spite of these pronouncements he was attracted to any woman, whether old or young, who had a good bosom, and he let me know it. When I would blurt out, "But that woman is at least fifty," he would respond, "She's an exception." I was almost convinced that thirty was not young anymore, when he took me with him on one of his nighttime prowls to the Place Pigalle. Here his favorite pastime was watching the "ladies of the night" and their business transactions. This was the moment of truth. We sat in a bar where the girls came back after they had turned their tricks. Between customers, they'd have a drink and sit around and talk. We got there about midnight and were so fascinated by the goings-on, we didn't leave until about 4 A.M.

What astonished me the most was that there were some relatively older women among the younger prostitutes. I particularly remember one of them. She was a sort of walking ruin, with deep lines in her face, a bright red mouth, and kohl-rimmed eyes. She was dressed in an expensive mink, her figure was so-so, and she led a tiny, woolly lapdog on an elegant leash. What particularly impressed me was that this person turned just as many tricks as did the younger women, that well-dressed men bought her favors, and that she kept it up all night, just like the others. Then, as the place finally closed for the night, neither her many customers nor her good humor left her.

"What do you say about that woman?" I said to my friend, deeply satisfied. "How does her success fit in with your theory that men are attracted only to women under forty?"

"Don't be silly," he answered. "This one is 'quality.' You can see that at first glance." And for him, that was that.

But not for me. That night, six years ago, the light finally dawned. *How can it be,* I thought, *that men are attracted only to young women, when I have just seen with my own eyes how men actually wait their turn and how they even pay to sleep with an old, obviously veteran prostitute?* I thought about it for a while. What *woman* would pay to have the honor of sleeping with a "used-up" man whom she had to approach in such a place?

There's another episode to this tale. Shortly after out visit to Place Pigalle, we had visitors. My friend's sister came to Paris and stayed with us for two weeks. She was a typical American "grass widow," married, with two small children and a nice house in the suburbs. She left the house only to go grocery shopping, to take the children to and from school, or to play bridge at a neighbor's. Otherwise, she knew nobody. Her contacts with the outside world were only through her husband. She lived in her world of television and was often depressed and felt old because "on TV they're always showing how men go after the young women." She herself was barely forty and not at all bad-looking. She told me she had trouble with her husband. She figured her age was the reason for her husband's neglect. In reality she had never really understood him—or herself—sexually. As far as she was concerned, everything about sex was distasteful. But I didn't learn about this problem until years later.

During the time she was in Paris I tried to cheer her up, but nothing helped. She didn't even like the story about the prostitute; she had never seen anything like that, she said. In her opinion, it was a man's world—one in which only teenagers were the epitome of what was desirable.

But this is not the end of the story. The best is yet to come. A short time after she returned home, the bad news arrived. Her husband had left her, seemingly overnight. The reason? Not an eighteen-year-old teen-bopper but a forty-eight-year-old (three years his senior) mother of four children!

One day I learned the truth about my Hungarian grandmother. She lived in a medium-sized town that is now part of Rumania but in those days belonged to the Austro-Hungarian Empire. She was the daughter of a well-to-do doctor who was head of the local hospital. She had a liberal arts education, was extremely talented, spoke four languages, and conducted a literary salon. She wrote and published poems, played the piano beautifully, and married my grandfather, a high-ranking Austrian army officer, when she was much too young.

As a child I was already afraid of my grandfather. In his later years he returned to Vienna and lived in a princely apartment where echoes sounded whenever you crossed the room. Every visit was formal, like a reception for a head of state. It was most upsetting. Grandpapa was completely unsuited to his young wife. He was also absent for months at a time, so nobody was surprised when he returned home after a three-month absence to find an admirer hidden behind the concealed door leading to his wife's dressing room. The ensuing scandal led to a duel and a complicated divorce. Grandmama took her three-year-old son, my father, back with her to her father's house. She began to appear on the stage, opened a bookstore that became the best in the city, married a professor from the local preparatory school, and in time became a widow.

I never met her, but she wrote me charming letters in perfect German, and for a time we carried on quite a correspondence. The answer to my question as to why Grandmama never came to see us in Austria was always the same: Rumania was behind the Iron Curtain, and she couldn't get permission to leave. At first this answer satisfied me. Later I found out that older people were al-

73

lowed to travel to the West without any difficulty. The correspondence between Grandmama and my father was always in Hungarian. The letters he received were always long, but he seldom translated them. Sometimes she sent pictures. I remember one of them exactly. It showed Grandmama in a beautiful garden. It was summer. She was eighty-four at the time and stood, a trifle stooped, next to a tall, attractive, blond young man who supported her lovingly. When I asked who he was, my father answered only, "Oh, some acquaintance or other." I didn't find out the truth until after Grandmama died—not long ago, in fact. The young man in the picture was my father's stepfather. Grandmama had married him when she was seventy-six and he was twenty. They were together until she died at the age of eighty-six. He has not remarried because, as the relatives tell it, she's the only woman he has ever loved.

My father knew about this the whole time, but he was ashamed of his mother and didn't say a word about her young husband. His relationship with his mother was never terribly cordial. He was raised by his grandfather and, more particularly, by his great-aunt, whom he adored. The duel, the divorce, and the attendant scandal overshadowed his childhood. His mother's marriage to a man fifty-six years her junior was more than he had the strength to bear.

For my brother and me, however, this news was fabulous. We were extremely proud of our grandmother. We debated the subject for a long time and found in her story lessons to be learned in our own lives; we saw proof that spirit and personality could triumph over body. I have a number of pictures of my grandmother as both a young and an old woman. She was never really strikingly attractive. She had beautiful curly hair, a very womanly figure with the obligatory tightly laced wasp waist, but she was no great beauty. Yet, everybody who knew her remarked on her sparkle and personality, discernible even in her letters, which are intelligent and full of humor.

What I used to know about older women and young men came only from reading about them in the newspapers or in books. (My mother was three years older than my father, but this didn't count.) I read about seventy-seven-year-old Englishwoman *May Goodman*, who had to go to America to marry her twenty-year-old stepgrandson, Mark, because they were refused permission in England. This, of course, was considered a quaint story, and so all the newspapers wrote about it.

I knew that *Anna Magnani* went around only with beautiful young men about the same age as her grandson. (Tennessee Williams writes about it in his memoirs.) I also knew about Austrian cabaret singer *Greta Keller,* known for her low, hoarse voice; she paved the way for *Zarah Leander* and *Marlene Dietrich.* Keller lived with a very young man, and when she died in his arms at the age of seventy-two, he was only twenty-six.

I also read about *Edith Piaf* and *Princess Margaret* of Great Britain, who both had had much younger lovers. But to discover a similar situation in my own family seened fantastic and exciting, extraordinary and stimulating.

As soon as I found out the truth about my grandmother, I began instinctively to look for other examples of women with younger men. I didn't have to go far. They were all there in plain view. American singer and show star *Dinah Shore* lived for six years with Burt Reynolds, eighteen years her junior. *Yoko Ono* was seven years older than John Lennon. San Francisco mayor, *Diana Feinstein,* actresses *Romy Schneider, Audrey Hepburn, Marisa Mell,* and

French nightclub owner *Régine* all have husbands or lovers who are many years their juniors. TV star *Diahann Carroll*'s late husband was sixteen years her junior. German actress and writer *Lilli Palmer,* ex-wife of Rex Harrison, has been married for thirty-three years to actor and writer Carlos Thompson, nine years her junior.

Upper-class women throughout Europe have often had younger husbands or lovers. *Lady Jennie Churchill,* mother of Sir Winston Churchill, had been widowed for five years when, at age forty-seven, she married the twenty-six-year-old George Cornwallis-West. They were happy for thirteen years and, even after they divorced, remained friends. When Cornwallis-West remarried, he did not chose a younger woman but one of Lady Churchill's close friends, the same age as herself. Lady Jennie Churchill did not remain single either. At sixty-four she married Montague-Porch, twenty-three years her junior.

Once I got really interested in the subject, older women and younger lovers were everywhere: Anthony and *Cleopatra; Eleanor of Aquitaine* (eleven years older than her husband, Henry II, whom she outlived by a decade); Mohammed, founder of Islam, and his first wife, wealthy widow *Khadija,* fifteen years his senior. The mother of Johannes Brahms was seventeen years older than his father. And she was not, as one might think, a "good catch" from a wealthy family, but rather a poor seamstress. The marriage was very happy and Johannes Brahms himself continued the tradition. He never married because all his life he remained passionately in love with *Clara Schumann,* Robert Schumann's wife, who was the most famous concert pianist of the nineteenth century. Clara was the mother of eight and was fourteen years older than Brahms.

The list could go on and on and on. French writer *Colette* married her third (and last) husband when she was sixty-two. Maurice Goudeket, who was fourteen years her junior, brought order into her finances and loved her dearly until she died at the age of eighty-one. And, of course, there was French writer *George Sand,* (whose real name was Aurore Dupin) and her famous liaison with Chopin, who was six years younger than she was. *Isadora Duncan's* husband, Russian poet Sergei Esenin, was seventeen years her junior, and even conservative, middle-class author *Agatha Christie* belongs on the list. When she remarried, it was to a man fourteen years younger than she was, the archaeologist Max Mallowan. They had been married thirty-six years when she died. The same age difference existed between *Alma Mahler* and her third husband, Franz Werfel. The list could go on indefinitely.

One really notable example is painter *Georgia O'Keeffe.* Her erotic colors are powerful and full of warmth, and her landscapes, in particular, are magnificent: *Red and Orange Hill, Clipper Near Abiquiu, Lake George, Crows, Dry Waterfall,* and the breathtaking *Red Poppy.*

Georgia O'Keeffe started painting at an early age and was thirty-seven when she married Alfred Stieglitz, the father of modern photography. In 1946, when O'Keeffe was just sixty, the Museum of Modern Art in New York City put on a one-woman exhibit of her work. The acclaim was overwhelming: Georgia O'Keeffe was recognized as the most successful woman painter in America.

O'Keeffe's prodigious creativity continued into her early eighties, when, disabled by diminishing eyesight, she gave up painting. At this time, a young man, Juan Hamilton, a talented potter, entered her life. Their close association for several years prompted rumors of a marriage, but both denied it. Whatever the exact nature of O'Keeffe's and Hamilton's relationship, it is clear that he helped revive her creativity and brought joy to her life.

She took up pottery and, with renewed energy, resumed painting.

Today, Georgia O'Keeffe, who is in her mid-nineties, continues to lead an active life, rising at dawn, rejoicing in the clear air, the sun, and magnificent New Mexico landscape around her. When people visit her, they are impressed by her vigor and vitality, and when they leave they have lost all their anxieties about growing old.

There are many more such marriages, love affairs, and living arrangements than you'd think, but, as the majority of these people have no contact with one another, they think they are the exception. For this reason they feel insecure. The women keep quiet out of consideration for their husbands, and vice versa. Of course, vanity plays a role, too. Most of the women married to younger men look young themselves, so that at first glance you often can't tell any difference in age. In our day, which of us is about to admit that she's ten years older than you'd guess? The real truth can be found only in the ledgers at city hall, but more about that later.

After World War I, successful marriages in which the wife was significantly older than the husband were fairly commonplace. Women of my mother's generation—that is, those born around the turn of the century—prove this point. These women didn't have many men their age to choose from; hundreds of thousands of the men died at the front during World War I. Most of these women had only two choices: to remain single or wait until a new generation of men was of marriageable age. If they chose the second possibility, they were generally already in their mid-thirties when they married, and the men were often as much as ten years younger.

I know a number of such cases, all of whom live, or lived, harmoniously. One example was under my very nose: one of my mother's best friends. She is now eighty-three and her husband is seventy. When they married, she was in her forties, earning a good salary as a book-keeper. He was a dance instructor who had just opened his own dancing school. Both were experienced at the time of their marriage and had seen what the world was like. They are still happily married, and you'd never know there was any age difference either physically or mentally. In fact, if one of the two tends to become jealous, it is he not she. A mature woman who feels secure in herself as well as in her career has no trouble attracting younger man. How does Audrey Hepburn put it? "A lot of men are looking for a mature woman of twenty or a young woman of forty." And although the women I've cited so far belong to the realm of glamor and are active either in films, television, on stage, or are members of the aristocracy, the combination mature woman—young lover can be found almost everywhere.

Practically all of my women friends in Vienna, Munich, London, New York, Los Angeles, and Paris have younger lovers. They did not go out in search of them. The young men found them. As a matter of fact, none of these women wanted a young man at first. They were looking around for partners their own age. But since most of them had been married before and were now divorced, they had a very hard time with men in their forties.

"Bill tried to dominate me in the same way my former husband had," a friend named Marty told me. "After two weeks I kicked him out. I simply could not stand any more of that routine. I want to be my own person. That's why I settled for Gregory. He is twenty-six and worships the ground I walk on. He would never dare to dominate me. On the contrary, he tries very hard to please me—in every way. And that's nice for a change."

The friend I just quoted is not in any kind of glamor business. She was a Los Angeles housewife for eighteen years. After her divorce she moved with her seven-year-old son into a small rented house in Santa Barbara. She met Gregory at her son's school. He was (and still is) one of the teachers there. He says he liked her from the moment he set eyes on her. My friend Marty was not so sure. After several months of one-sided courtship, she gave in and they started dating sporadically. After the disappointing episode with Bill, however, their relationship became serious. Two years later, Gregory moved in with her and the boy. They have now lived together for four and a half years, and all three of them seem very happy. "I'll never let her go!" says Gregory with determination.

"You know," she explained later, "the young men of today are different. They are more sensitive. They don't have to prove all the time that they are stronger, better, more intelligent, and more successful than you are. For the first time in my life I live in a real partnership. Of course, you can't expect mink coats and diamond rings, but you get a lot of tenderness. And you realize that times are changing. Gregory's generation, for example, is much less promiscuous than the generation my former husband belongs to. When he was young it was chic to seduce as many women as possible, never mind whether or not you loved them. But the young men of today don't think that way. First of all, it is so easy to find a woman who will sleep with you; there is no more quest. Secondly, these men grew up with women's liberation. So the emphasis has shifted from seducing women for the sake of scoring to pleasing women sexually. And that is the advantage they have over older men. Men in their fifties and sixties are physically still in very good shape. But they grew up in a kind of sexual desert when women did not dare speak their minds. Before I met Gregory I had a short interlude with one of my former husband's friends. This man did not even know where to caress me. He could never find the spot where it felt good for me, thinking all the while he was wonderful. The lovemaking lasted for three minutes flat, and afterwards he had the nerve to ask me: "Are you happy now?" This man has been married for twenty-five years. I am sure he has never satisfied a woman in his life."

Nearly all the women I interviewed for this book, women living with younger men, told me the same story. The young men were more eager to please than the older ones. They were not tongue-tied in bed. They asked whether what they were doing was right. They were more concerned about the woman's pleasure than about their own. But more about that later.

As I said before, not only rich, powerful, glamorous, or aristocratic women have decided to give younger men a chance. Perfectly ordinary people do the same—and have been doing so for a long time.

Alain and Chris live in Paris. Chris is an Austrian woman in her fifties who has lived with Alain for a long time, though he is seventeen years younger. When they met in Paris eighteen years ago, he was twenty-three and she was forty. Chris had been divorced twice. Her first husband was an Austrian businessman; the second an officer in the French military. Her two children by her first husband both live in Paris. Alain and Chris met while they were employed by the same international firm. Chris is now head of payroll, and Alain is a computer programmer. When I first met them five years ago, they lived in the small loft of a beautiful old house in the historic Marais district. Chris owned the apartment, which was tastefully furnished and just big enough for the really exquisite dinner parties the two of them put together at regular intervals.

Since then they have moved to a larger apartment that they purchased jointly, but in the same area. The mere fact that they were able to live happily for ten years in the relatively cramped quarters of the smaller apartment suggests the strength of the bond between them, however. Their temperaments work in their favor. Alain and Chris are both extremely good-natured people. They have a glow about them, and people always have a good time with them. They are usually the focal point of any get-togethers, and Chris makes people laugh for hours, literally. She is not a beautiful woman, but she is blonde and stately, with a good figure, and she radiates unbelievable optimism and enthusiasm. She doesn't know the meaning of being afraid of age. When she retires, she wants to go back to Austria, if possible to Tyrol, and start an organic garden. Alain is enthusiastic as well and has already begun boning up on the technical aspects.

Alain and Chris enjoy a real partnership. The rhythm of their life is even and pleasant. Alain usually gets home two hours before Chris. He does the shopping and prepares the meals. Chris cooks on weekends and does the wash. They share the cleaning chores. They live well. They travel quite a bit, usually first class, and they throw expensive parties. Alain is happy that Chris is financially independent and is not at all envious of her professional success. Chris says Alain is the first man who has never tyrannized her.

They have had their problems, of course. When the company sent Alain to Germany for six months during their second year together, within three months' time Alain had an affair with one of the secretaries. Chris went to Germany and presented him with a choice. When he couldn't make up his mind immediately, she did it for him. "Stay where you are," she ordered him. "I don't ever want to see you again. This kind of affair will do you good. Obviously with me you haven't learned a thing about being responsible. Don't call me and don't write to me. Goodbye." He was back within three weeks, and there have been no similar incidents since.

Is Chris afraid of younger women? "Absolutely not," she told me. "Alain has since learned he can't replace me so easily. My being older gives me many advantages. I have enough self-assurance that I don't cling to him. I am strong enough to say to myself that I can live without him if need be, that the world wouldn't cave in, that I wouldn't have any money problems living alone. And I know that when I'm seventy I will be able to find another man, if I want to, and I sometimes let him know this."

When I returned to Vienna from Paris, I lost touch with Chris and Alain. Then, last year, we met in La Coupole, a café in Paris. We decided that Chris and I would meet at four o'clock and Alain would pick us up for dinner. Chris was on time, but she looked old and tired. I was shocked, and thoughts of infidelity, and separation raced through my mind; but that wasn't it. Chris had just gone through two operations and had been out of the hospital for only three weeks. "It was a terrible year," she told me, "but something good did come out of it. Do you know what? I'm now convinced Alain really loves me. In all of our years together he's never been more sensitive and loving than he is now."

Other friends, Kathy and Gerd, live in Cologne. Kathy, an American, has just turned forty-six. Gerd, her German husband, is twenty-nine. They both visited me in Paris to celebrate Kathy's birthday. It was an instructive evening. Kathy is small, wiry, and quick. Her ancestors came from Italy. She has a dark complexion and short, straight hair. Her first husband was an American university professor, by whom she had two children.

She met Gerd ten years ago. He was one of her husband's students. Two years later, Kathy got a divorce, took her children and went with Gerd to Germany, where they were married. Since neither one of them wanted any more children, Gerd had a vasectomy.

Kathy is not a professional. She is a housewife to the core. In the beginning they had money problems. But Gerd soon found a good job with a chemical company, and now he's planning to go into business for himself. They live in a very nice house on the outskirts of Cologne with a view of the Rhine. There are no problems between Gerd and the children.

There *were* problems, however, between Kathy and Gerd's fellow workers. They were accustomed to spending all night playing cards or to sitting for hours in their favorite local bars, and they expected Gerd to do the same, while Kathy sat quietly at home. But they didn't reckon with the fact that Kathy, as an American woman, was not going to tolerate such goings-on as a European woman might.

"If I had been twenty, I would have killed myself," Kathy says now. "But I was so indignant that, for every night he left me alone, I stayed away for a night. Of course I was only with friends, and I spent one night in a hotel, but he never knew where I was. After the fifth time, he had had enough. We made peace, and today he knows just how far he can go. He doesn't torture me any more. He knows how much it hurts to spend the entire night waiting up for somebody. He also knows that colleagues are no substitute for a family."

Kathy's greatest strength is her willpower. If she wants something, she goes after it like a butting ram, and most of the time she gets what she desires. She can also get on your nerves, of course. She loves to talk and will prattle on for hours, but she is still good fun. Sometimes, too, when going out for the evening with her husband, she gets into the car and sends Gerd back into the house twice because she has forgotten her gloves or her necklace. "Oh, the poor man," she then says, truly sympathetic, as he returns. Despite this, however, she is a stimulating, interesting, and amusing person. Gerd bears up with unbelievable patience. I once asked him why.

"Because she's unique," he said. "Because I've never been bored with her for a second. Because I appreciate her housekeeping. And because she is the best lover I ever had."

Now for general testimony. At the beginning of this century we may have been prudish in many ways, but there was one thing that was common knowledge: A mature woman made a much better sexual partner than did a younger one. For centuries young men's first sexual experiences were mostly with older women. Shortly before World War I, the young Agatha Christie was being introduced into society. She was a debutante in Cairo and swore that the dashing officers had eyes for the maturer ladies only: They had their sexual fun with married women, usually a good deal older than themselves," she tells us in her autobiography. "I did cast languishing eyes on a handful of bronzed middle-aged colonels, but most of these were already attached to atractive married women—the wives of other men—and had no interest in young and insipid girls" (New York, Ballantine, 1978).

What those men knew then was forgotten for a while, but now it is surfacing again: *Older women are better lovers!* Masters and Johnson have come to the same conclusion, rediscovering only what the ancient Greeks already knew: Women take longer to develop their full sexuality; their best years begin in their thirties; older women and younger men are by nature perfectly suited to one another.

I remember the last interview Henry Miller gave for German TV shortly before he died. He talked about love and life and women, and ended on a note of praise for the mature among us. "The woman whom I loved most in my life was older than I was," he said. "I met her when I was seventeen. She was twice my age. It was the best relationship I ever had." And he went on to recommend to other men what writers, artists, and painters already know— namely, that older women can teach younger men an awful lot of valuable insights. That it is a blessing to be loved by a woman who is generous, understanding, and mature. That every man with any sense should try it."

So why should women be afraid? Science has proved that we get better with age. Nature has been very kind, sparing us a terrible ordeal: the fear of losing our sexual potential as we grow older.

When men slow down, women get better. It must, however, be said in all fairness that a lot of men keep up pretty well. My own family is evidence of this. Men can be fantastic lovers at any age—if they have the right partner.

But back to the disadvantages of being a very young woman. What is wrong? First of all, her body is not yet ready. A woman under twenty cannot ordinarily be swept away by an embrace as a woman of forty can be. Usually,

86

she does not even like her own physical appearance. She will be full of inhibitions in bed. Isn't she too flat-chested? Aren't her legs too thin? Her hips too fat? So, instead of concentrating on her lover, she holds in her stomach, afraid he might find it too protruding. Because she is so scared, she is usually much too tense. Sexual movements don't give her too much pleasure yet. As a result, actual lovemaking is not that satisfying for her physically. So she feigns orgasm to get it over with. At least, that's what I did at that age.

Since she doesn't really like her body, she prefers to make love in the dark. So she and her partner are truly in the dark, physically and mentally. She feels those hands on her body, but she doesn't dare open her mouth and say: "Please, not here, a little farther up," or "You hurt me. Not so hard." Worse than that, she is incapable of saying sweet little endearing things to the man. She expects them from him, of course, and later puts them down in her diary. I remember it all so well.

What a relief to be a mature woman. So many fears gone for good. The mature woman has learned to like herself, and her greatest asset is that she is no longer afraid of a male body. I remember well my first experience with a naked man. It was uncomfortable and frightening. And when we're afraid of something, we can neither love it nor be good to it. Naturally, a man senses whether his body is accepted and desired, or whether it is rejected. And, naturally, a man wants to be spoiled, stroked, kissed, admired, and loved—just as a woman does. If a man lives too long with a woman who rejects his body, he'll become impotent, just as a woman in a parallel situation will become frigid.

A mature, sexually awakened woman is always alluring. As a teenager, I lost several admirers to an older relative.

87

And I know of two cases of a daughter's lovers switching to the mother, with whom the relationships lasted significantly longer. Not only will a younger man find sex more physically satisfying with an older woman, but he also finds understanding and security with her. The combination of mother and lover is an unbeatable one. The Greeks knew all about this, and for that reason they meted out terrible punishments for incestuous behavior. The playwright George Bernard Shaw had something of interest to say about this theme. Lilli Palmer repeats it for us in her autobiography *Change Lobsters—and Dance*. " 'I always wanted to rewrite *Oedipus,'* Shaw said. 'Now then, tell me, why should that fellow Oedipus get into such a state when he finds out that he's married to his mother? It should have added to his affection.' "

The sexual relationship between an older woman and a young man is, in fact, almost always more honest than one between an older man and a young woman. If a young woman sleeps with an old man, she can fake arousal and desire even if she doesn't feel a thing and is disgusted by his body. A good lover notices this right away, of course, but there are many men who don't and some who even think the ecstatic moans of a prostitute are real.

A young man who sleeps with an older woman, on the other hand, is putting his cards on the table. He can't force his body to make love. If her body is distasteful to him, he won't achieve an erection. Those who claim that young men live with older women only for financial gain can be easily silenced. The true test of the intensity of the relationship comes in bed.

Young women who read this shouldn't misunderstand me. Nothing is further from my mind than to increase the insecurity most inexperienced women feel. On the contrary, I want to give them a comforting glimpse into the future. I want to reassure them when I say that at seventeen, eighteen, nineteen, or twenty, they have not yet experienced the best of which they are capable. I want them to look forward to their forties, fifties, and beyond. I want them to realize that the best is yet to come.

Basically I want to tell the young not to let people scare them. When I was sixteen, everyone tried to convince me that, as a woman, I would be over the hill at twenty. It was criminal. And it was wrong. Because, with every year, my life has become better. Therefore, by stressing the advantages of those who are mature, I want to build up the self-confidence of the young. And young people need this so badly. Nothing is finished at twenty or forty or fifty, believe me. Don't hurry into a marriage at twenty-five because you have been told that at thirty you'll be too old. Don't rush into a job that means nothing to you because you are afraid five years from now nobody will want you. I studied until the age of thirty-five. *And I found a job the first day of my search!* If I stress in this book the advantages of the older woman, I want at the same time to provide arguments with which to counter people who try to put women down. Do not believe them. Age will enrich and, in many cases, also beautify you. Nature has given women very good bodies. And they are made to last a long, long time.

Now back to those city-hall statistics I mentioned earlier. The fact is that, since the beginning of the 1960s, marriages in which the woman is older than the man have risen sharply. In 1975, in West Germany, the woman was senior to the man in one out of every seven marriages, and in the United States in one out of every five. In the entire Western world, more and more older women are marrying younger men. In England, in the 1960s, statistics showed that such marriages had risen by 15 percent since the postwar period. Now it is 20 percent, and these marriages are lasting longer than those between partners of the same age. Municipal archives reflect similar trends.

That liaisons between older women and younger men are increasing is already clear in the minds of the population experts. Birth records tell the story. The public is not aware, for the most part, that all over the world, ever since statistics have been compiled, 6 percent more male babies are born than female. Perhaps this is nature's way of compensating for the higher death rate among newly born males. Before World War II, baby boys used to die in great numbers. In the last forty years, however, medical science has made such progress that the infant mortality rate has been reduced to a minimum.

The result is a surplus in young men. One English government report, published in *Time* in 1979, shows that in the United Kingdom alone, there were 1.3 million men but only 789,000 women in the twenty- to twenty-four-year-old age group. That is to say, there were half a million young women too few. In the twenty- to thirty-four-year-old age group, there were nearly 800,000 fewer women. This means that in England alone there were nearly one million young men who would not be able to find a partner of exactly the same age. Need I say more?

Two more considerations on the subject of older women and younger men. Do not worry about wrinkles. "If I were living with a younger man," a woman friend said the other day, "I am sure I would get up early in the morning to put on makeup before he wakes up."

What nonsense. A man who is attracted to a mature

woman knows that her skin won't be as smooth as a baby's bottom. And he usually does not care. I've noticed this again and again. Younger men are much less frightened by little signs of aging than are older men. Young men are not put off by wrinkles. They don't have any themselves yet, they haven't started thinking about them, and they do not feel in the least bit threatened by them. Many older men feel the same way, but there are some who are vain, who hate to discover those little lines on their own faces, and for this very reason they do not want their women to have them. Some older men definitely hate to be reminded of their age, so they surround themselves with teenagers.

A young man who likes mature women likes them for their warmth, their knowledge, their experience, their generosity. Wrinkles are perfectly all right, if you tell the truth about your age. If you have lied, however, if you have told him that you are twenty-five when you're forty, matters are more difficult. Remember: Never try to pick up a young man who is not interested in you. If you are looking for a young lover, mix naturally with young people and wait until one of them comes to you. Never pretend that you are as young as they are. This is fatal. Be your own self, be proud of your age, wear it as an adornment. If you kowtow to the young, you are cheapening yourself.

One last word: Some people said to me the other day, "Well, living with a much younger man is certainly all right in your middle years. But what about old age? Won't the difference be too telling?"

You can find that out for yourself. Try and get hold of some photographs of Salvador Dali, the Spanish surrealist painter, and his wife. He is seventy-eight; she is eleven years older. If you see those two seated together, you won't notice any difference. But if you were to see them walking together, you would, although not in the way you might expect. As soon as they get up, she looks ten years younger than her husband. Because it is she, the nearly-ninety-year-old, who supports him!

4

My Own Sexual Development

I was all of twenty-four when I married. I had hardly said "I do" when suddenly I felt old for the first time in my life. I was always used to having a circle of friends around me, including a couple of admirers I usually kept at arm's length. Now, here I was, a married woman, living in London without a single friend. My husband had no friends either. Except for a couple of "old boys" from his school we were invited to see every two or three months, and of course my in-laws, we saw nobody.

My husband was English. The better I understood his language, the more hopeless the situation became. I found I didn't love my husband, that he was very different from what I had thought, and that all the hopes that had arisen during the period when we had communicated in broken sentences, gestures, and looks remained unfulfilled. I began to suffer dreadfully from homesickness and had my first bout with depression.

Sexually, we didn't understand one another at all. This was nobody's fault. We both simply had had too little experience before we were married. We were incredibly naïve and had never heard about "chemistry." After only one year I no longer wanted to sleep with him. I didn't find his body repugnant; it was simply a matter of total indifference to me. I felt nothing at his touch. In spite of this, however, I became insecure and uneasy if he didn't want to make love to me. The physical act of sex seemed to me as much a part of my wifely duties as cooking and doing the laundry. I always took my duties seriously and wanted to do everything the right way, exactly as it was expected of me.

I was twenty-four years old, newly married, and life should have been beautiful. But it wasn't. I was bored to death. To compensate for this I began to stuff myself. As soon as I got home I went straight to the kitchen. There was a blue stool there. I sat down and had the refrigerator, breadbox, and cookie jars within easy reach. One after the other, cheese, paté, cakes, chocolates, and what was left of lunch went into my mouth. Once, I remember, I baked a cake with whole hazlenuts and ate it, still warm from the oven, at one sitting.

I managed to live with this for two years. How I did it I don't know anymore. I only know that there was no joy left in my life. In the morning I didn't look forward to the day ahead, and in the evening after work, I did not want to go home. The thought of seeing my husband again didn't do anything for me, and I certainly wasn't looking forward to the night. During my entire marriage I never had an orgasm.

Then, during that rainy, rainy summer, my mother came to London to visit. She looked at me and said, "You don't exactly look happy." Over the next three days we talked about nothing but my marriage. "If you want to," my mother said to me on the fourth day, "get a divorce. You can always come to live with me. But one thing you should know: Sexually, there's still hope. Maybe you are just too young. Many women are not capable of enjoying a man until they're over thirty. Before that, very often the body just doesn't function correctly."

After my mother had left I went to a gynecologist who told me the same thing. "Don't give up," she said. "You'll be able to survive these few years until your body is ready. Then everything will be better."

Even as I was still thinking about this, my mother-in-law invited us to visit her for the weekend at her beach house. We were very happy to be leaving London, and we were looking forward to the fresh air and good food. My in-laws had a dog, a cute black and white spaniel, as well as a big garden with roses of all colors and a luxuriant mulberry tree.

Tea was served every afternoon punctually at five o'clock. The whole family gathered in the salon, the beautiful antique silver tea set stood on the table, and there were delicious cakes, hot scones, and tiny cucumber sandwiches. On this particular weekend the weather was good and the men went sailing. My mother-in-law and I were left alone. We drank our tea peacefully and talked.

Among other things, we discussed the fate of a twenty-five-year-old niece named Jill, who had no plans whatsoever to get married. She had no specialized education, changed her job frequently, and only once had brought a boyfriend home to introduce to her family. That had been three years ago, and nobody had seen him since.

"Don't be upset," I said comfortingly. "She'll find a husband." And to convince her, I told her about an American acquaintance who had married for the first time at the age of forty-nine and whose husband was a well-do-do German landowner with large tracts of property in Brazil.

"Oh, you Austrians," my mother-in-law said, "you are really refreshing. You have such a healthy way of looking at life, and you're so optimistic. We English could learn a lot from you. I was brought up to believe that once a woman is twenty-five her life is behind her."

All day Sunday I thought about my mother-in-law's words. I compared them with what my mother and the London gynecologist had said. How could people like my mother-in-law think a woman's life is over at twenty-five when experts say that her sexual drive is only just getting off the ground? I was confused and decided to keep my eyes open from that point on. I began to take note, particularly of myself.

No matter what has been written about a woman's sexual growth, I know I was not capable of desiring a man physically until I was past twenty-five. I was really mature only at thirty, and, if I hadn't moved from Austria to France at the tender age of twenty-one, I might never have matured at all.

Throughout my entire youth in Austria I was terribly hurt and embarrassed by the way my classmates talked about physical love. The vulgar jokes the boys told to try and arouse us only made us sick. The boys who used these shocking four-letter words in my presence were, as far as I was concerned, finished. I would never talk to them again.

To make an American understand this seemingly exaggerated reaction to sexual slang, let me explain that the German language is particularly unsavory in this respect. Most words created by the Germans and Austrians for certain parts of their bodies are downright disgusting. If you want to talk about sex in German, you have to use medical language.

Let me give you an example. In English you can say: "I want to make love to you." In German there is no such expression. Either you start talking in Latin, or you point in silence to your bedroom, hoping that he'll understand.

Nice parts of your body are debased by ugly designations. Do you want to know the German word for "nipple"? Hold on to your chair. It is "breast wart." "Give me your breast wart, darling." Would that turn you on? I doubt it!

I know that sexual slang exists in all languages. There are horrible words in English and in French, but in those languages you also have an alternative. In French you can talk about the most intimate sexual matters at a formal dinner party without offending anyone. If, for example, someone discovers that, after a night in a seedy hotel in Pigalle, he has caught a certain kind of insect, a tiny louse that tries to make permanent a home in his body hair, he could converse openly about it, because the French, patronizing anything to do with love and sexuality, have invented a very pretty word for it. You know what they call it? "Papillon d'amour," which means "love butterfly." (Don't ask me for the German translation.)

The Germans, in my opinion, are lousy lovers. People are like the language they create to express themselves. If they love a thing, they will not invent foul words to describe it. So much for sexual slang in Austria and Germany. It made my youth pretty miserable.

I was seventeen when I slept with a man for the first time. He was a well-brought-up and sensitive boy. Despite this, I was so shocked by what happened, by the fact that another body moved into mine and by the way in which it moved, not to mention the pain it caused, that for the next year and a half I didn't allow a man to come near me.

As a result, I helped to perpetuate the poor opinion men so often hold of women because of their own unfortunate youthful experiences. I did what most young women do to strengthen their self-confidence and test their powers over

97

the world of men. I went dancing, wore low-cut dresses, flirted like mad, went on dates, held hands, and let myself be kissed. But my waist was the utter limit! Not an inch farther! Sorry, darling. I was scared of sex but fascinated by the maneuverings that went on around it, the hot breath, the moans, the trembling fingers, and the effect achieved by pressing my stomach against a certain part of the male anatomy. I didn't realize that I was teasing the man. I felt no desire to make love and had no idea how frustrating it must have been for him when I'd plead, "Please, stop now."

If the man then started to admire my superhuman self-control, I had no idea what he meant. My body simply was not ready. I felt no desire. Up to the time I was twenty-one, I could lie stone cold for a whole night, completely naked, next to a young man trembling with desire. No spark would spread between us.

I had my first serious relationship at the age of nineteen. My friend was the same age. We saw one another two or three times a week, and whenever there was an opportunity—we both still lived at home—we slept together. What I most liked during those nights we shared was the warmth of his body, his desire, and his tenderness. The rest I simply let pass. Sometimes we didn't see one another for two weeks at a time. Even if I missed his presence, I didn't miss his body. In spite of this, I was convinced we had a big sexual thing going since, with him, lovemaking didn't hurt anymore.

Had I remained in Austria, I probably would never have progressed beyond this point. That Germanic society's hostility toward the body and the incessant sexual allusions made me withdraw more and more from men. When I came to France, new dimensions opened up in the truest sense of the word. I suddenly found myself surrounded by people who were proud to have a body. All at once physical love was beautiful, and you could talk about it without blushing. It was heaven! I also found, to my great surprise, that sexy jokes don't have to be vulgar but can be charming and erotically suggestive. After a year in France I was considerably healed from the wounds received in Austria. I was twenty-two and promptly fell in love with a Frenchman.

This was a very important step in my life. For the first time, the physical act of love was not just something to be tolerated but a pleasant experience. For the first time, I found it normal for two people to want to sleep together. For the first time, I didn't have to invent excuses, rely on white lies and delaying tactics. For the first time, I wasn't afraid. I told him I'd sleep with him. The only problem was where.

Jean-Pierre was my student. He was nineteen and needed German lessons in order to be accepted at a university. The first time I saw him he was standing at a window with his back to me. He turned around as I shut the door. We looked at one another and something happened. As early as the second lesson, we knew that we wanted to sleep together, and we both admitted it.

Even so, it was two whole months before we could spend a night together. I lived in a Catholic home for girls, and he still lived with his parents. Neither of us had a friend with an apartment we could use. Going to a hotel was out of the question. The only thing left for us was wild kisses at parties and during taxi rides. It was purest ecstasy— driving through Paris while pressing against one another and losing ourselves in the warmth of our bodies. I never knew where we were going. All I remember is opening and shutting the taxi doors. During the day we met in various small cafés, mostly in the back room, which in

Paris is often one flight below street level. There we would nearly devour each other.

Then quite unexpectedly, after Christmas, I found an apartment. I had been looking for half a year and had all but given up hope. A French acquaintance who worked as a beautician and shared an apartment with an American had been transferred to Monte Carlo, and I was left her room. The house was on the rue Pascal. It was one of those small, shabby old Parisian houses with an inner courtyard and a female *concièrge* who was always drunk. Today there's a new housing development on that site.

The old house had two floors and our apartment was upstairs. It consisted of a combined kitchen-living room with a sleeping niche and a living room with another sleep niche. The toilet was in the hall and consisted of a cube-shaped block of cement with a hole in the middle. The American had installed a hand shower in the kitchen. She worked as a secretary, and in the evening she sang American folk songs at a club behind the Church of St. Germain des Prés.

It was in this apartment on the rue Pascal that at the age of twenty-two I spent my first night of love. For the first time, I wanted to feel another's body in mine. A sleepless night, or *nuit blanche,* as the French say. I didn't reach orgasm, but I didn't care. The discovery that a man's movements could be pleasant and arousing outweighed everything else. I felt I was a woman. I was convinced I had reached the absolute heights of sexual fulfillment.

And yet, whenever Jean-Pierre wasn't there I didn't miss anything. Once he was away on a trip, and we didn't see one another for a whole month. Of course I was looking forward to seeing him again, but not for sexual reasons. I did not know then how strongly women could feel about sex. But I knew something else: That women were supposed to get married in their twenties. So I started looking for a "safe" man. At the age of twenty-three I found him and left Jean-Pierre for my English husband, whom I mentioned earlier.

The prophecies of my mother and the London gynecologist came true. At twenty-seven I had my first really satisfactory affair with a man. It wasn't, as you may guess, with my husband. Anthony and I met at a time when I really wanted to die. My marriage had become unbearable. My husband and I didn't fight, but we didn't have anything to say to one another either. Each time my husband tried to touch me, I became cold as ice. I developed such an aversion to his body that one day when he came out of the bathroom wearing only his pajama top I was nearly sick. I had given up all hope that things would get better. I was convinced I was frigid.

I met Tony at a dinner party. We just happened to sit next to one another, and we hit it off at once. He was tall, blond, and sensitive; he worked as a real-estate broker and was about to go into business for himself. We talked for hours about music and animals and decided to see one another again. Shortly before the end of the evening, he found out I was married. "Too bad," he said, and left abruptly. Four days later, heart pounding and with a very bad conscience, I called him. We met the next Saturday (my husband had gone sailing), went to dinner, then dancing, and finally ended up at his place.

After my first night with Tony I knew this was what I had been waiting for. I also discovered I wasn't frigid. When I had known him for a month and a half, I left my husband and moved in with him. During those first days with Tony, everything changed—the world took on more color and every minute was exciting. I dropped twenty-five pounds without effort. I spent hours in front of the

101

bathroom mirror, admiring my slim figure, daydreaming, recalling every minute of the night before.

This was not a one-sided relationship. I was able to desire that man as much as he did me and it was an astonishing revelation. For the first time I felt as excited as my partner did. I wanted his body just as badly as he wanted mine. It was fantastic. Suddenly I understood what the Bible means when man and wife are described as being of "one flesh." I knew my friend's body as well as I knew my own. Whenever I touched him—and for the first time in my life I felt the need to touch and kiss him everywhere—it was as intense a pleasure as if I myself had been kissed and fondled by him. I was now able to give as well as take. I could finally stop pretending arousal and feigning orgasm.

As so often happens in life, everythings started to happen all at once. Bad news seldom comes by itself, they say. The good as well, when it bears down upon us, does so from all sides. While my first two years in England had been cold, rainy, and gray, this summer was sunny and hot. In London, the women wore sleveless dresses. We went walking along the banks of the Thames barefoot and sat until eleven at night on the wooden benches lining the streets outside the pubs. The small, round, carefully pruned trees on the street outside Tony's house flowered as never before, and when they dropped their petals the sidewalks turned into a beautiful white carpet. We went to concerts and spent intermissions on the balcony of Queen Elizabeth Hall looking down at the river. We bought a fondue set, experimented with all types of sauces, and invited people over. We spent weekends in bed with no desire other than to lie next to one another and feel the other's presence.

Nevertheless, a year later I went back to Vienna to complete my studies. But we kept in touch. We wrote, called each other often, and spent all our vacations together. During the long weeks I was in Vienna without him, sometimes as long as two and a half months at a stretch, I was quite busy and completely faithful to Tony. I missed him terribly and counted the days until we could be together again. Otherwise, I felt good and was not overly plagued by erotic desires.

Today, at the age of forty, I can live contentedly by myself. But, after a month, I want a man badly, even when I'm not in love. I want to feel the warmth and strength of another body. I want to make love. If this is impossible, I have erotic dreams. This started when I was thirty-five and has intensified over the past three years.

It feels great to be sexually mature. And for the last few months, I have suddenly been experiencing a new kind of orgasm. When I was very young, orgasm was simply a nice feeling. Now, however, it is phenomenal. Not every time, of course, but sometimes.

I never knew that orgasm could "go to your head." Yet this is precisely what happens. The sensation not only envelops my whole body, it keeps on going up and up until I experience this overwhelming ringing sound in my ears, which leaves me incredulous and very happy. Maybe this is nature's present for my fortieth birthday. I certainly won't complain.

So much for my physical development from teenager to mature woman. It took over twenty years, and only today can I say I am really able to understand men. Before I knew what physical love could be, I thought of most men primarily as nuisances. I could not sympathize with their physical desires. When I read Hemingway and his description of a time of crisis in Paris when he could neither write nor sleep with his wife, I wondered about his praise of his wife's understanding, her endurance of his impotence, and her great patience. *What does he mean by "great patience"?* I thought. *She is probably only too happy to be left in peace for a while!*

Whenever a man wanted to approach me, I thought him lascivious and couldn't understand why he was so hurt when I turned him down. Now I know that mutual sexual desire is absolutely imperative in any partnership. You can, as a woman, fake sexual pleasure; and the younger you are and the less you feel, the louder you moan— remember? When this continues over a long period of time, however, the relationship will do a lot of harm to both partners.

Every woman can learn to feel physically free. Most of this process can be left to nature, which matures and prepares the body for sex. But you have to be ready to do your part as well. Perhaps women who have had problems similar to mine should go abroad for a while. As a foreigner, you'll benefit from a kind of fool's freedom. In a new country you can develop in a freer atmosphere than in surroundings where everybody knows everybody else and you feel under constant scrutiny. The fear of losing your "good reputation" is gone, and you can experiment, look for a partner who pleases you, free from the pressures of either parents or friends.

The greatest advantage of growing up, both physically and mentally, is that you lose the fear of the opposite sex and know approximately how much you can expect. In their youth, boys and girls are nearly enemies. Each one wonders just how much he or she can get out of the other. How much love and tenderness, how many hot meals and clean shirts, how many clean windows and floors, how many children can she give me? How much love and tenderness, how high a standard of living, how much security can he offer me? If they marry too young, both often have the feeling they've drawn the short straw in the exchange.

Mature women are usually less self-conscious and closed off from the rest of humankind. They are more able to see beyond themselves. "Do you find it normal," my husband once asked me, "for me to have to sit in an office every day from nine to five?" I looked at him in astonishment. Of course I considered it normal. Furthermore, as far as I was concerned, he earned far too little money. Sometimes he seemed like a racehorse I had bet on but that left the starting gate too slowly. I found it perfectly normal that he wasn't enthusiastic about his work, that he sat around dissatisfied and on Sunday evenings sighed, "Oh, God, tomorrow is Monday again." This was the world of work men had created for themselves, and it was not of my doing. I felt free of any responsibility, and, if there was a victim, I thought it was me, not him.

Today I feel quite differently. I find it unacceptable that men heap burdens on themselves, tormenting themselves with responsibilities, until they collapse from a heart attack. Both partners have to make an effort. Dependence on money ruins one's character. It is so degrading to ask for a pair of new shoes. The financial dependence many women accept as part of their "wifely role" also leads to an emotional attachment that has nothing to do with free choice. The dependent partner is constantly afraid of being abandoned, and love then smacks of a contemptible, slavelike devotion.

The mature woman who supports herself is free from all of this. She can accept things in good conscience because she knows she doesn't *have* to accept anything at all. She can say yes to an invitation to dinner without even a twinge of guilt feeling because she knows she can always reciprocate. If she is financially independent, she can ask for the best from her partner, even in bed, if she too is willing to make a total commitment.

It is an unbelievable relief when you discover, somewhere around your thirty-fifth birthday, that you can rely on your own judgment. You spare yourself much disappointment. Above all, you stop wasting precious time on men with whom you have nothing in common. Think of the evenings we spent (when we were younger and didn't know any better) with men who were unsuited to us. We struggled for hours to keep a conversation going, searched frantically for topics that would interest the man, paid compliments, laughed at unfunny jokes, and, finally, when nothing worked, felt this terrible sense of failure. At forty, some things are easier. One glance and a woman knows: *This man is not for me.* On the other hand, after half an hour with another man, she may know something quite different: *It might work between us.*

Mature women have the best chances of finding men suited to them. A woman who is financially independent and has acquired a certain amount of knowledge of human nature is not about to settle for second or third best. Of course, some women are lucky, marry at twenty, and are quite content for the rest of their lives. But the chances are one in a thousand. Two hundred years ago it seemed to have been even worse. The English writer Mary Wortley Montagu thought it was more like one in ten thousand and urged her granddaughter to remain unmarried. A woman whose marriage has broken up and who has the strength to support herself also has the energy to look for just the right person and not act out of fear or desperation. A woman who stands on her own two feet is not about to cling to a bad partnership. She is strong enough to say,

"I'd rather be alone for a while than have a relationship that goes against my nature."

For this reason, late marriages often last longer. By the time you're thirty-five or forty, you know what to expect. You are able to be creative personally and in your work, and you feel no need to force your partner into the role of permanent savior. You also know you're not missing anything by being faithful to your husband or lover if the relationship is good; you are too experienced to risk that love for a mere fling.

I think the majority of men prefer mature women to young ones. Last year, world-famous jazz guitarist Barney Kessel came to France. After a sensational performance and a standing ovation, he showed me a photograph of his new wife, Joanna, whom he had married just two months earlier. Barney looked great at fifty-eight and so did the woman in the picture. She had a beautiful complexion, long straight, black hair, a slim figure, and the kind of expression on her face that makes you happy by merely looking at it. "She is fifty-three," said Barney, glowing with pride; he said it in a way that made you realize that he considered her age an asset—just as friends might show you a beautiful watch and then add, *"And it is real gold!"* Barney is, of course, right to be proud of his wife's age. If a person looks that lovely at fifty-three, her beauty is going to stick.

If you talk to people, if you keep your eyes open, if you look around and analyze what you see, you will realize that society is changing and that the advantages of growing older are being more and more recognized. And why shouldn't they? Finally you are getting to know yourself. You have gained self-confidence. You know what is good for you and what isn't.

A mature woman knows she belongs to herself and that nobody will be in a position to suppress her personality, as is so often the case when we're younger. She knows that what counts in life is honesty, diligence, and benevolence. She knows from her own experiences that when she works hard and carries out her responsibilities, she has little to fear. And she will have discovered that good men are responsive to these qualities of character. Older women are also learning to ignore many of the commonly accepted social boundaries. They are beginning to take even younger men and their attentions seriously. Mature women are no longer always looking for a provider. Often they prefer a lover. If you look around, you'll find that women over forty have never been so admired by younger men than they are now.

I wouldn't want to be eighteen or twenty-five again. I'm very happy to be forty, but I wouldn't want to stay that age. I know that the most beautiful and most important half of my life is still ahead of me. I am prepared for, and looking forward to, it.

5

In Praise of
Mature Motherhood

We need know-how for everything we do in life, and that includes being a mother. Of course, children are quickly conceived and somehow grow up in spite of what we do or don't do. But to bring them up to become a joy to their parents and responsible members of society, takes patience, experience, intelligence—in a word, maturity.

A child who has mature parents is lucky. A woman who doesn't become a mother until she's thirty or older usually knows what she's doing. She probably already has both feet on the ground and has completed either her professional training or her schooling. She knows what responsibility is. She lives in a house or an apartment in which she is comfortable, whether she is married or not, and is likely to be more confident in her dealings with the world and, in particular, with men. If need be, she can raise her child alone.

A mature woman will never let her child feel that he or she stands in her way. She has had time enough to dance the nights away, to go on vacation when it pleased her, to fall in love, to flirt, and to prove herself as a woman. She knows she hasn't missed anything really vital. She knows the sky won't fall if she can't have an evening out—in contrast to the young mother, who becomes desperate when she can't afford a baby-sitter. She hasn't had her fill of parties yet and is convinced she'll be missing the most exciting parts of life out there in the world. And, consciously or unconsciously, she'll make her child suffer for it. A woman who doesn't have children until she's between thirty and forty-five is also more relaxed. She does not get upset over little things and knows that a happy child is more important than clean clothes. She may even laugh over a broken lamp because, at her age, she can afford to buy a new one without having to cut drastically into her monthly budget. She has a stronger will than a very young mother and will defend her child against anyone, if necessary against her own husband.

The reason so many young mothers overreact to the noise or the confusion surrounding their children is that they are afraid of their husbands, who are probably just as young and going through their own period of trial and error. Just a year ago I witnessed this with my own eyes. I visited an acquaintance in Düsseldorf. She was only twenty-one, had married at nineteen, and had her daughter shortly thereafter. Her husband was a salesman, three years older than she, and he came home just as we were having coffee.

He washed his hands, and the first thing he said as he came into the room was, "the bathroom looks like a bunch of thieves have been living in it." Gerlinde jumped up guiltily. I went with her. The bathroom wasn't messed up at all, except that there was a small yellow toy car next to the door and a hand towel lying on the edge of the bathtub instead of being hung on the rack.

As we came back into the living room, her husband looked disapprovingly at the "construction" little Natalie had carefully and happily put up around the coffee table. Without saying a word, Gerlinde began to pick up everything. The child's crying was ignored. Soon the sobs became louder, the husband quieter, and Gerlinde more nervous by the minute; the child was scolded and sent to bed.

All Gerlinde's husband had to say was, "In an apartment as small as ours there has to be some semblance of order; otherwise we simply can't live here." The apartment was a renovated attic. There was only one large room, and the sofa converted into a bed. The child's bed was placed behind a screen. But there was a full bathroom and an ultramodern kitchen. The kitchen was Gerlinde's husband's pride and joy. "I really broke my back in order to buy you this kitchen," he said whenever he wanted to get his own way. He constantly blackmailed his wife with the kitchen and the long hours of work it had cost him, and it always worked. Gerlinde was "only" a housewife and overflowing with guilt feelings complicated by the fact that she had persuaded her husband to marry her because she was pregnant.

People should have children only because they really want them. Children are too precious to become a means to an end. It is criminal to have them either because one wants to catch a man (which usually goes afoul anyway), to save a faltering marriage (which never works), or to stave off boredom and fill your own inner void.

As soon as the children are there and the desired result hasn't been achieved, the tragedy begins. One form the tragedy can take is called child abuse, and there is an increasing volume of research on this subject. In Europe as well as in America the story is the same: Young fathers and mothers are much freer with their hands than are mature parents.

"Young mothers are responsible for eighty-five percent of all child abuse cases," an official of the U.S. Health Department told a reporter for *The New York Times* four years ago. "We have about a million cases reported a year. Of these, two thousand end fatally. These are grim statistics. But one thing we do know: If we could only persuade women not to bring any more unwanted children into the world, and, in general, to wait a couple of years longer before they begin their families, then we would soon have the problem under control."

Until recently, women over forty were instilled with a fear of difficult births and the possibility of having children with Down's syndrome. Now, the greater concern has shifted to the problems created by young and immature mothers and fathers. Statistics have shown that, of the children incapable of finishing their basic schooling, 75 percent were born to mothers aged twenty or below. Findings have been similar for juvenile offenders. Seventy percent of the children charged with arson over the past few years were children of teenage mothers. You also find the largest percentage of premature and still births among young women under eighteen.

For decades, birth defects were blamed almost solely on the mother's age, just as for centuries mothers were falsely held solely responsible for the sex of a child. Only in relatively recent times have the fathers been taken into account, lifting the burden from the women.

Professor Andreas Rett, an Austrian scientist who has studied the parents of more than 2,000 children with Down's syndrome, has conclusively proved that in one-third of the cases the abnormal tendency was atrributable to the father. "The cell-division process that is responsible for mongolism can take place not only in the egg but also in the sperm cell," says Rett. "A number of scientists have suspected this for a long time, but we've only just gathered sufficient proof. The father can be the cause just as easily as the mother."

Rett has also pointed to an increase in the frequency of mongoloid births in Europe after the war, particularly in the families of men who had been prisoners of war in Siberia. The risk of begetting a child with Down's syndrome was considerably higher if the father had suffered years of starvation and hard labor in Russia. As for the mothers, the risks increased when the child was conceived shortly after either another birth or an abortion. The mother's age made little difference. Half of the mothers of the children in Dr. Rett's study were young.

Throughout the ages and among all peoples, women have borne children as long as they were fertile. Were it "unnatural" for the mature woman to have children, wouldn't nature have ended her childbearing years at thirty and not carried them into her forties and fifties? Many women don't enter menopause until they're between fifty-five and sixty. In large families, before the advent of the pill, late babies were a common and often welcome occurrence. As the "nestlings," these babies were the darlings of the family, fussed over and spoiled, and were often twenty years younger than the firstborn. To try and convince healthy women in their mid-thirties or early forties that they are no longer "whole" women and that they run a far greater risk of bearing abnormal offspring is something quite new. My mother's generation never heard of it. Its development runs in a parallel vein to the youth cult of the postwar period, which is exactly when it started. Thank God, this notion, along with the Lolita culture, is on its way out. Today one often hears of forty-year-old

113

women giving birth. And, even better, it is now more often considered unnatural to force women to have all the children they want in their early twenties.

In 1979, Dr. Mildred Scheel, a famous physician and former First Lady of West Germany, talked with me about older mothers. Dr. Scheel, who had her first child when she was twenty-nine and her second in her late thirties, warned about paying too much attention to those statistics that instill so much terror in mature women. "Those statistics," she said, "have been compiled only over the past few years. There is no historical evidence. Many such observations were collected from the far corners of the world. . . . Ninety-nine percent of the time they pertain to women in the developing countries."

In many of the countries of the Third World, social security, government subsidies, and pensions are unheard of; children are the only security parents have against old age. The more children they have, the better the parents will be cared for. At least one or two of the children will survive, they think, to take care of them in their old age. This—and the general scarcity of reliable birth-control information—goes far in explaining why so many "women" become mothers when they are still adolescents. A woman who has her first child at fifteen and, during the course of her marriage, goes through countless pregnancies, cannot, at age forty-five, be compared to a European woman who has benefited from contraception, better nutrition, and better general health care, not to mention a higher standard of living.

Significant numbers of Western women who are professionally successful first but don't want to forego having children are deciding to start their families when they are in their late thirties or early forties. This trend started at the beginning of the seventies and continues to intensify.

Among the actresses who have set examples are *Sophia Loren,* the late *Natalie Wood, Claudia Cardinale, Romy Schneider, Catherine Deneuve, Susannah York,* and *Marietta Hartley,* who had her children at thirty-five and thirty-eight. An overjoyed *Ursula Andress* announced in January 1980 that, at the age of forty-three, she was expecting a child by her friend, a twenty-nine-year-old American actor. She now has a fine baby boy.

Nobody thought it extraordinary for the Swedish queen, Silvia, to have her first child in her mid-thirties. I met her, by the way, during her last state visit to Vienna in 1979, and she is now pushing forty, a mother of two and more beautiful than ever before.

In the United States, many studies exist of women who had their first child when they were over forty. Countless articles appearing in newspapers and magazines recount their experiences with motherhood. As early as 1972, *The New York Times* interviewed a number of mature mothers, among them: a forty-seven-year-old interior decorator who had thought she was infertile but had a healthy son after twenty-six years of childless marriage; a university professor who married at thirty-two and then purposely postponed having a child until she was forty-one in order to establish herself professionally; an actress who gave up her career in her late thirties and suddenly, after eleven childless years, found herself pregnant at thirty-nine. A number of women also interviewed had had unhappy first marriages and hadn't met a man with whom they wanted to have children until they were over the age of forty.

Whether they were working women or not, all of them agreed on one thing: Pregnancy, childbirth, and the experience of living with the child represented an unbelievable enrichment of their lives. Their doctors were impressed by the women's bravery; none of them showed

115

even a trace of self-pity. "Women who have their children later in life not only stay young longer," a Manhattan gynecologist noted, "but they make excellent mothers. They experience motherhood with much more awareness than younger women. They don't complain. They don't get excited at every little thing. They know how to live. They give their children more freedom and raise them to be much more self-reliant because they have more experience and fewer fears than young mothers."

"Children of older parents are more intelligent," at least in the opinion of well-known Rumanian gerontologist Dr. Anna Aslan. She was on her way to a congress in South America and stopped off last spring in Vienna where we talked. "This is no miracle. Older mothers have more of everything: more time, more self-confidence, more brains, more money, and more responsibility. This has to have positive results."

It's a well-known fact that children of older parents do better in school. The jealous world of onlookers has even produced a word for them: precocious. That is what we call children who know more than their playmates of the same age. Although the description is often meant as a criticism, it is basically a compliment. We can't ever be too smart, and the younger we start, the better.

Why do children of older parents have an easier time of it? Quite simply, because they get useful answers to their questions. My mother was forty-two when she had me. During my entire childhood I never once heard my mother say, "Don't ask such dumb questions." If I wanted to know something, it was patiently explained to me until I was satisfied. I got all the help I needed, whether it was in my homework or with my piano lessons. I had the advantage of receiving advice and pointers on living that young mothers can't give simply because they lack the experience.

I also never heard, "Not now. I don't have time." My mother always had time for me, although she ran the household and worked part-time from the time I was seven years old. I had a very happy and secure childhood. My mother's age didn't present any problems. She picked me up from school as all the other mothers did their children, and it never occurred to anybody to say, "Your mother is older than mine." The topic never came up. The only difference between me and my schoolmates was that I trusted my mother with even my most intimate secrets. I knew she understood me.

The greatest advantage in having an older mother is that you yourself lose the fear of getting older. When I was ten years old my mother was fifty-two. She was sporty, full of vitality and humor; as far as I was concerned, she was a young mother. When I was twenty, I discovered that a woman of sixty-two isn't old either, and now, at forty, I know there is no reason for me to fear the age eighty-two.

Another important point—a mature mother is often more candid about her child, feels less threatened by her growing son or daughter. While a young mother may be anguished to have an already grown child, the mature mother is happy to have a teenager still at home. And the child knows the difference. The problem can go deeper, too. A young mother wants to be young. She is young, looks young, and wants to be thought of as young. The children, however, are visible proof that she isn't as unencumbered as she'd like people to think, that she is no longer a young girl but already a woman with duties and responsibilities. Of course, there are many young mothers who have no trouble overcoming these problems. But there are enough who do, and I'll give you an example.

In Paris I knew a painter named Claudine. She was extremely attractive, had a delicate face, a tiny body, huge brown eyes, and an elegant walk. Claudine lived in an apartment that was the essence of artistic taste. She had the right clothes, her husband earned a good living as a fashion photographer, and, together, they personified what is meant by "beautiful people."

When I first met Claudine she was thirty-six years old. She sometimes picked me up from the library; I can still see her today, the way she stood in the entrance, leaning on the wall. She was dressed in blue jeans, slender as a young boy, a peaked cap on her head; she was young, fresh, and seemed to be without a care in the world.

Claudine gave frequent parties, and people clamored to be invited. She was the perfect hostess and always had the right mixture of people together. Her parties were invariably entertaining, and her small, long-haired dachshund, called "Mrs. Quickley," never failed to provide the unexpected. He'd hide himself behind the long drapes and emerge, with loud barks, at the most inopportune moment. In the summer he would do the inevitable on the balcony so that it dripped onto the street below. In the winter he occasionally did it on the living room carpet when he found he wasn't getting enough attention. He was a very affectionate dog!

Claudine had but one bad fault: She told lies! In particular when it came to her age. Only those women who had known her for years knew that she was over thirty. Most of her acquaintances thought she was in her mid-twenties. One summer she gave a party to which she asked about forty guests, among them a young poet, who read some of his works.

It was nearly eleven o'clock when suddenly the door to one of the guest rooms opened and a pale young girl of about fourteen appeared and looked around, searching. Claudine jumped to her feet, as if a firecracker had exploded under her chair. She grabbed the child by the shoulders, pushed her back into the room, and shut the door behind them. Ten minutes later she came out again.

"Who was that?" I wanted to know.

"Only my niece," Claudine replied.

"Why don't you let her listen to the poetry?" I asked.

"Because she has no understanding of it and would only be a nuisance."

Later, in the kitchen, as I helped carry large platters of salad and shrimp with rice into the dining room, I mentioned to Claudine's husband that I hadn't known they had a niece visiting. "We don't," came the answer. "Claudine lied to you. The child you saw is her daughter from her first marriage. The way she treats her will cause us to break up yet. But I won't say anything more. Normally, the child is away at school, but it's vacation time now. Day after tomorrow she'll go to her grandparents. There at least she'll be treated like a human being."

Claudine is perhaps an extreme case, but there are many young women who are not capable of taking on the responsibilities of being a mother. They seem actually to fear the word "mother." Their children dare not address them either as Mama or Mother or Mum but are told to call them by their first name as if they were just another acquaintance. What children lose by this, they'll never understand. After all, there is for each of us only one person in the world we can call "Mother."

A woman who asks her children to call her Susan or Jane is only prepared to play the role of a friend. "We are best friends," the woman says. But children don't need additional friends. They have enough friends at school. They need a support, a grown-up who protects and cares for them but who also teaches them, through his or her example, discretion and consistent behavior. A child loses trust in a mother who pretends to be on his or her same level. Children don't consider it an honor at all when parents not only tell them their troubles but also, when possible, ask for the children's advice.

Such behavior can only place more stress on a child already overburdened with growing-up problems. Children are much more fragile than one thinks. Parents who forget to protect their children from unnecessary cares, who only want to be friends, not parents, often end up raising neurotics. The friendly relationship generally doesn't last very long. It collapses, at the latest, at the onset of puberty. The daughter develops into a little woman who, as often as not, is full of her own problems and has to prove to herself that what her mother can do, she can do better. Now the fight begins. The young mother is too young herself to tolerate competition from another woman in her immediate presence, and suddenly the friends become rivals.

This phenomenon can be witnessed time and again. It is terrible for the daughter and tragic for the mother. Not far from where I live there's an elegant, divorced woman sharing an apartment with her two daughters. She is in her mid-thirties, the daughters are fifteen and seventeen. The mother married at eighteen because she was pregnant. As a result, she had to abandon her dream of going to school and traveling around the world as a foreign correspondent.

The rivalry that exists among these three women is so intense that it is embarrassing even for an outsider. The mother feels constantly compelled to make up for her lost youth by showing she has more success with men than her daughters. Of course she does, but this doesn't satisfy her. At every opportunity she tells you how often people mistake them for sisters, that she has exactly the same figure as her older daughter and wears her clothes. She tells you how she has never "played mother" to them, and that both girls have been responsible for their own personal development.

In the course of the last four years the mother has incessantly changed boyfriends. Her daughters have stopped bringing their dates home because the mother invariably starts an affair with them. For revenge, the girls make overtures to the mother's lovers, and the fight is on.

Both girls have done poorly in school. The older daughter has left home, after first going to live with her father. After only two months she moved into an apartment with her boyfriend and has broken off all contact with her parents. The younger daughter is still at home. Not long ago I met her on the street with her mothers. Both of them were loaded down with groceries, as they had just gone shopping for the weekend. The daughter arrived at the door and rushed in first, tearing the shopping bag out of her mother's hands.

"Can't you be more careful?" the mother called out angrily.

"Oh, Annette, shut up," her daughter answered. So much for "mother as best friend."

Another acquaintance, whose daughter was born when she was twenty-two, simply can't stay away from celebrations, whether they be birthday parties or other of the girls' gatherings. And each time she acts more childish than the young people present.

Children suffer when forced to bear the brunt of their parents' neuroses. I recall the mother of one of my dance-school partners. When I met her I was sixteen and she was forty-four. In her youth she had been a famous figure skater, until she married at age seventeen. Her husband was nearly thirty years older than she and had a good job as a high-ranking civil servant. She had her first son at the age of twenty-three; two others followed.

The family owned a weekend house near Vienna. I was invited there. The first thing the mother of my dance partner asked when she saw me was, "How old are you? Seventeen! When I was seventeen I had been engaged for a year already." Then she took up my time by recounting, non-stop, her youth and her great successes in the skating rink. In between, we drank tea, ate cake, and looked through boxes filled to the brim with old snapshots of sports events.

Throughout the entire weekend, she never stopped mentioning the great difference in age between her and her husband, and did everything to prove that she came from a younger generation. She let no opportunity pass to emphasize that, if the truth be known, she belonged to the generation of her son and me. Shortly before dinner on Saturday night, we were discussing bathing suits. "Come," she said to me and her son, and we followed her into her bedroom. There, to my amazement, she stripped completely and began trying on a series of bikinis. She asked our opinion, gently rocking her very attractive hips back and forth. Today, I realize that she wanted to hear compliments on her excellent figure—but then, as a seventeen-year-old still shocked over her peculiar behavior, I was not able to make them. I didn't even realize what she was asking of me.

That woman was a typical victim of a badly arranged life. Skilful, ambitious, and more successful than her friends because of her prowess as an athlete, she had wanted to have it all too soon! It wasn't until she married that she realized she had made a mistake. As she began to consider what her life would have been like if she had finished her schooling and became a professional instructor or a trainer, she became very dissatisfied. Her husband noticed this and developed an inordinate jealousy. He had gone into retirement, was constantly home, and began to watch her like a guard dog. He noticed at what time she went out to do her shopping and what time she came back. If he thought she had been out too long, there were angry words. Once he caught her gossiping with one of the neighbors. Because she hadn't come back home to him right away, he locked her in the cellar for two hours.

She told me this, not indignantly, but as proof of how much her husband loved her. I don't think she realized what else came into play here: Parents lock their children up. In this case she was the child and obviously she liked herself in that role.

Her own relationship with her children was not the best. Her sons were proud of her beauty but didn't take her seriously, and none of them would have dreamed of going to her for help with a problem. The oldest son committed suicide after a short and unhappy marriage. The second son became an engineer and emigrated to Canada. When her third son finally made her a grandmother, she hadn't the slightest desire to see her grandchildren. Today she's sixty-four years old, a handsome widow with a good pension; but she still laments her lost youth.

Mature mothers are generally spared all of this. They seldom resent their offspring or feel they've missed something by becoming mothers. The bond of a mature mother to her young is usually very affectionate and trusting. In addition, the "empty-nest syndrome" doesn't happen with older mothers. The mothers know that they are needed up to a very advanced age.

Lots of women are simply not ready for motherhood at twenty. As American actress and TV star Marietta Hartley told *Harper's Bazaar* for their 1981 issue on women in their prime, entitled "Over Forty and Sensational," she could never had had her two boys in her early twenties. Only at thirty-five, she recalled, did she feel ready. Before becoming a mother she had problems keeping her weight down. She loves French food and adores eating it. After her second son was born (she was then thirty-eight), she suddenly realized that she had no more weight problems. "Having those kids really made a difference," she smiled. "I panicked when I was thirty. And you know, I used to be much heavier. But after my babies, my metabolism changed. It was as if my body said, 'Thanks, I needed that!'"

If you talk with young mothers of small children, you inevitably hear that "when the children are grown" they're finally going to do this and that, be able to afford more, take trips, get their driver's license, go back to work, and earn money. . . . As much as these mothers love their children, they still talk about a time when the children will have grown up as a time of their own release. This attitude, that motherhood basically means bearing a heavy burden from which one will eventually be freed, has its pitfalls.

At an international congress in Rome three years ago I met a woman from New York. She was about forty-five, had married young, and had had two children between the time she was twenty-two and twenty-four. She had gone back to work three years before we met, and talked very reluctantly about her life as a housewife and mother.

What really shocked me was the sentence, "When I was a mother, I had absolutely no money, and that's the reason I want to forget that period in my life."

She had used the past tense: "When I *was* a mother. . . ." Here was a woman who considered herself a mother only as long as the children lived at home. For eighteen long years she had done her duty, but not one day longer. Once the children were gone, she put aside everything that had to do with being a mother, and turned her whole energy into making up for what she had missed.

What was her relationship to the children now? "Normal," she said. During the school year both of them live in a university town. They work during summer vacations to earn tuition money, and they are home only at Christmas, and sometimes not even then. They both have plans for the future. The daughter wants to go to California. The son, who is younger, wants to go to Europe when he has finished school.

Isn't she hurt that the children want to go thousands of miles away to settle down once they can fly on their own? No, not at all. "America is a huge country," she said, "and the people are mobile. I know of hardly any family where children of twenty still live with their parents." Nor did she know of any young people who wanted to spend an evening out with their mother or who went, voluntarily, on vacation with their parents. And that's the way *she* had behaved toward *her* parents. Once a year she went to see her mother, on a duty visit, and that would have to do.

The fact that she spoke of her children as if they were two heavy attacks of smallpox she had endured is a tragedy in itself. No wonder so many Americans feel so insecure. Children are still children at eighteen. A twenty-year-old needs his parents' help and advice, and even at thirty, when we're just beginning to understand the world, we're not too grand to refuse a helping hand now and then. A mature woman understands this, and she wants her children to be around as long as possible. She will never say "when I *was* a mother." She *is* one. And she is proud of it.

More and more, sociologists, psychologists, teachers, and doctors (especially women doctors) agree that the best time to have children is not between twenty and thirty but between thirty and forty. A child psychologist recently asked, "Why should a woman take on an irksome burden at twenty when she can do the same thing purposefully at thirty-five?"

"I don't know," a young mother of four children said. "They say we should start later, but later one doesn't have the nerves for it." This is a fallacy. Any twenty-seven-year-old who already has four small children to care for might not have the nerve to start all over again at the age of forty. But people who have had it relatively easy between twenty and thirty, who never had children before and do want them now—these women *do* have the nerves required for the task. And a lot of valuable experience on top of that.

Now a few words about professional life. A very young woman who stops working in order to raise her children only a short time after she enters the work force often finds it difficult to re-enter her profession later. She probably didn't work long enough to specialize in one field or another, and the time at home has left her isolated so that it is more difficult for her to become reaccustomed to the work discipline. This can, of course, be overcome, especially by a woman who brought discipline and order to her home life. Self-confidence may be the more difficult obstacle to clear.

But if a woman has settled in a profession, if she has built something and stayed at it until she is in her mid-thirties, it is unlikely that one or two years away from the job will endanger her career. She has already become part of the operation. If she is self-employed, she has her clients. She has shown that she is capable, and she will be taken back joyfully. She may even be able to create a position that will allow her to divide her time, so that neither profession nor child is neglected. Very probably she will be able to hire help for the most time-consuming household chores.

What conclusions are we drawing from all this? First of all, those women who have no desire to have children at the age of twenty-five can confidently have them ten years later. Secondly, don't be ashamed if you don't want to be a mother at all. Few people today look askance at a woman because she has no children. A great rethinking process has begun. The human race is in no way threatened with extinction. On the contrary, the world is in danger of overpopulation. Even a nuclear war couldn't kill all of us. Therefore, the new motto is quality, not quantity; better to have fewer children, raised with love and care, than more, raised with resentment; better to become a late mother than to be a young one who beats or neglects her offspring. Having children is something wonderful. Only a mature person can properly understand it and recognize that giving birth is a miracle of creation, not a simple everyday event.

Any woman who, despite the drawbacks, still wants to have her children when she's young should make sure she completes some kind of professional training beforehand. The more you learn, the more you have to give to a child. Youthful enthusiasm isn't enough. A child also needs intellectual guidance. The false advice that young and in-

127

experienced parents sometimes pass on to their children is a genuine drawback because it will stick with them not only throughout their school years but possibly throughout their entire lives. Prejudices can be instilled quickly, much more rapidly than you think.

Finally, an amusing example. Our neighbor had two grown sons. At the age of forty-seven, she suddenly had stomach trouble and bouts of nausea. She went to a doctor, who treated her for ulcers. When nothing helped, he told her that in all probability she was going through an early menopause. Five months later she had a healthy baby boy, with no complications.

While I was still talking about this case with my family, I found evidence that in earlier centuries many women had their first babies at forty. The grandmother of the famous English writer *Mary Wortley Montagu,* who lived in the seventeenth century, hadn't married until she was forty-five years old. She then started a family and after her children were born, until she died at the age of ninety-five, she was a sought-after, brilliant society lady. I also found out that *Frances Burney,* a writer of romantic novels, who lived in the eighteenth century, married a French military officer at the age of forty and gave birth to her first son at the age of forty-one. While I was doing this research, the good news we had been waiting for came from New York: An acquaintance, married to an American, had finally had the child she had wanted for so long, and the child was a girl, just as she had wished. The mother was fifty years old, and this was her first child. I had met her in Rome while she was pregnant. An exceptionally beautiful woman, she was "radiantly pregnant" and seemed to have been ennobled through the child she was carrying. The birth came off with no complications. Mother and daughter were and are healthy. The child is now three years old.

Late motherhood can do no harm either physically or mentally to a healthy, dedicated woman. On the contrary, women who become mothers relatively late seem to blossom through their children and stay young longer. Children benefit from having a mature mother in that they are more likely to receive a purposeful start in life. And, finally, later motherhood is one solution to a problem that besets many clever and creative women: how to balance career and children. Women used to feel they had to choose one or the other. Now, there is no need to forego either. It is simply a question of how you structure your life.

6

Old Age and Loneliness; or, All About Grandmothers and Terrific Old Ladies

Getting old is like being on a trip and seeing the mountains rise up in the distance. Perhaps you think you'll never be able to cross them, the car won't be able to negotiate those formidable heights. So what happens? The closer you come, the less forbidding the peaks look. The roads level off beautifully, the car moves easily over the highland that seemed so threatening. Your fears were groundless.

My mother, as I've already mentioned, is eighty-two years old. This would be regarded by many as an advanced age. When one is with her, however, and hears her laugh, experiences her vitality, the absurdity of calling her old becomes apparent. My mother thrives on life, much more so than many younger women, and this despite the ordeals experienced in two world wars and their horrors: hunger, inflation, bombings, and fears for the safety of her husband and children.

My mother does not live in the past but in the present. When the Iranians started to force women out of the universities as soon as the mullahs took over, and when the Russians occupied Afghanistan, it was just as terrible to her as it was to me. She is very much part of our time. This, in fact, keeps her young. And she *looks* young, because she doesn't consider herself old.

Not long ago we talked about life, births and deaths, about getting older, and about life's expectations. What did my eighty-two-year-old mother have to say? She declared with conviction, "I have absolutely no fear of growing old." My mother is lucky, too; she seems to have an "aptitude" for living. She is even-tempered and enthusiastic. She has kept her spontaneity. She is still able to stop in the middle of a long walk to admire a chestnut tree in full bloom, and as she does so her eyes light up. Her joy is infectious.

When she wants to go to the opera and can't get a seat, she buys standing room. This upsets her friends, who keep asking, "But don't you get tired when you have to stand for such a long time?" "Of course not," she replies. "The music is much too exciting and, besides, I can sit down during intermission."

Looking at my mother, I have come to realize that a person changes very little during the course of his or her life, and is no less lovable at eighty than at eighteen. She still has the same kind of energy and, when she really wants to do something, she'll get it done without delay just as she did when she was a young woman. There is one concept she absolutely doesn't understand, and that is the notion of a "lonely old age."

"Lonely old age" is a slogan for our times. It's no worse really than just plain loneliness, although those who coined it certainly meant it to be. If you look at it closely, loneliness has nothing to do with age. People who are lonely are those who cannot bear to be alone, and being young or old makes no difference.

Everybody knows that loneliness can be a problem even in young people; it can even be detected in children of

131

kindergarten age. Some children can play by themselves for hours at a time. Others pester you every ten minutes with, "What can I do now? I'm so bored," even when they're surrounded by the most beautiful toys.

Naturally, a gift for being alone is, primarily, a question of talent. A bright child can do more with a chest full of building blocks than can another child with little imagination. The ability to be alone without suffering also depends to a great extent on the parents and whether or not they taught the child that it is nice to be alone from time to time.

Last year while on vacation I saw a classic example of how the fear of loneliness was instilled in a small girl. I was sitting with a group of friends on the hotel terrace after dinner. We were making "grown-up" conversation, and my friend's eight-year-old daughter began to get visibly bored. She was very good about it for an hour or so, but then she wanted to go back up to her room to play.

At this point, her father was deep into a discussion of gasoline-efficient cars and didn't want to be interrupted long enough to take the child upstairs. When the child pestered him a second time, he washed his hands of the whole matter. Assuming his most authoritative voice, he said, "You really are a little dummy. Why do you want to go upstairs? You'll be all alone up there, do you understand? All alone. Here you're with us, and that's so much nicer. Who wants to be alone in their room?"

How it all ended I don't remember. But his words angered me to such an extent I remember them vividly to this day. How can anybody consciously encourage in a child the fear of being alone? How can anybody lead a youngster too immature to make comparisons into such false values, in this case convincing the child that the company of people with whom she has nothing in common is more important than her own company? It's depressing for anyone, child or adult, to spend an evening in the company of people you have nothing to say to. Everybody is familiar with the overwhelming feeling of boredom that descends on you when, for business or other pressing reasons, you are forced to spend time with people who are not of your own kind. So you drink too much at these dinners, cocktail parties, or other social occasions, and afterward you feel sorry. Isn't it a hundred times better to be alone, to plan a pleasant evening, to be able to think, to write letters, to take a bath and wash your hair, to practice an instrument or listen to music, to talk to friends on the telephone, to cook a gourmet meal for yourself, to map out plans? How marvelous it is to be alone after, say, the turbulence of the holidays or big family get-togethers, to have time for contemplation, to rest up.

I have spent entire weekends alone with the greatest of pleasure, especially when I had lots of work to do. I don't *want* to see anybody when I'm busy or, to be perfectly honest, when I'm in the middle of a really fascinating book. Once I spent two whole days in bed reading Thomas Mann's *Magic Mountain*. Another time, I stayed home for an entire weekend with Wilkie Collins's *Woman in White*. I remember, it was lovely weather and everybody I knew was at the beach, but I stayed home on my ivy-covered kitchen balcony, lying on blankets and pillows, a cup of coffee next to me, being blissfully happy, not wanting for anything or anybody. As far as I'm concerned, I *have* to be alone from time to time. I need time alone as a period of regeneration.

Of course, it helps if you come from a family in which people are not afraid of being alone. My mother, who has her hands full with six grandchildren, is always happy to have a few days of peace and quiet by herself in her own apartment after a strenuous weekend with the family. Then she doesn't like to be disturbed and lives according to her own routine, getting up when she wants to, cooking what she likes, reading, watching television, and going to bed when *she* decides to do so. For her it is easy, because she knows that she can be with people whenever she chooses.

The people who love her, however, and desire her company didn't simply appear out of the blue. She has a large circle of devoted friends and family, but this didn't just happen; she has earned their affection. Always be on your guard when you hear stories that begin: "Yes, when I was young there was always something going on. I was invited here and there, and I had so many friends. But, now that I'm old, nobody wants me anymore. I'm all alone because of my age."

In general, anybody who was popular and active in her youth will be so in old age as well. Anybody who has a pleasant personality, who is intelligent and sincere, who is sympathetic to and will stand up for others, will be as welcome a guest in old age as in younger days.

For many years my mother lived in a small town in upper Austria in a five-family house. Four of the families were always fighting among themselves. They fought over the garden and the fence and whose turn it was to shovel snow. The two families who lived on the ground floor didn't speak to one another for years. Their children were even forbidden to play with one another. . . . And who became the mediator? My mother. She got along with all of them and didn't let herself get involved in any of the intrigues. She gave in on unimportant little matters that the others always magnified into new complaints, and was generally beloved everywhere. Not only were her neighbors happy to talk to her and invite her into their homes, but *my* friends from school considered her a number-one mother, too.

An admirer from my dance-school days used to visit her regularly years later, after he had been married for years and had children of his own. My girlfriends preferred to come home with me to my mother for advice. And today, whenever they see me, they send her their greetings and ask how she is. When I'm invited to their homes, they always add, "And bring your mother with you." As for her own contemporaries, she has many friends among them, too. She has remained in close contact with her best school chum for sixty-five years. What is so special about my mother? The answer is simple: She is good fun and she never complains.

Unfortunately, there are too many older people who have nothing to talk about except their various ailments. It doesn't matter what other topic of conversation you bring up, they always come back to their aches and pains, never tiring of describing these in the most excruciating detail. It's not that they are fascinated by the subject of illness. Oh, no. Most of them don't even want to listen to similar tales of woe from their own contemporaries. It is, rather, a question of priorities; the only thing they care about is themselves. There is nothing more important than they and their lives; nothing interests them beyond their own person. They need others only as grateful listeners to the one and only all-encompassing theme, "Me, myself, and I."

After fifteen minutes, at most, in the presence of such people you get very depressed. What are the consequences? You avoid their company. It's no wonder they complain about being alone. Yet, they are the cause of their own misery. Such egotism can lead to nothing else. It is their selfishness, not their age, that drives people

135

away. Of course, the roots of their conduct lie in their youth. There are plenty of twenty-year-olds who can talk about nothing but themselves, and, when they happen to let the other party get a word in edgewise, they're not listening but thinking, *What should I say next?*

These people will always be unpopular no matter what their age. When they are young, the problem isn't all that obvious; if they belong to a group or club—a chorus, a dance class, an athletic team, or a school organization—other people in the group serve as buffers. But once they are grown up, they're alone, because they have not been able to form one single true friendship, one that will last through the years.

Nothing in life comes free of charge. If you want to take, you have to give first. If you want people to talk to you, you have to make an attempt and draw them into the conversation. You can't prattle on for hours about your own concerns, boring those opposite you to tears, expecting that they will like it and come back. They won't. If your attitude is to sit back expectantly waiting for the world to come and amuse you, you'll soon be alone for good.

Of course, if you're wealthy enough, you can buy companionship. Instead of good fun and stimulating conversation, you can offer people dinner parties, expensive wines, and invitations to play tennis or spend the weekend at your country house. But don't make the mistake of thinking these people are friends. They come to you because they want to enjoy the luxury, and not because the host is such a marvelous person.

Unfortunately, nowadays position and social standing are often held in higher esteem than good character. To my mind, this is another reason so many lonely old people exist. If you make it professionally, you have not yet made it on a personal level. You might often be invited, but mainly for the services you might have to offer or because people do not want you for an enemy. But as soon as you retire, as soon as you have no more power, you'll be in for a shock. Invitations will be slow in coming and there won't be a single "friend" left.

It is very interesting to see how our values have changed. If you read novels written earlier in our century and compare them to those written now, you'll know what I mean. For example, if the qualities of a son-in-law are described, the older books put the emphasis on personal accomplishments. Of course, to have money did no harm; after all he had to support a family. But also a matter of general concern was whether or not he would be able to *live* with this family he wanted to start. If a mother examined a suitor for her daughter, she always wanted to know: Is he of gentle disposition? Is he good-natured? Does he have a sense of humor? Can he play an instrument? Is he good to animals? Is he a good storyteller? Is he good company? (The two most important questions—Does he drink? Is he a gambler?—had already been asked before she invited him into her drawing room.)

In our day and age all people seem to be interested in is: "Does he have a lot of money?" And, if he does not, "Is he aggressive enough to earn it?" It does not seem to matter whether or not this man is a pest as soon as he comes home to you after his aggressive day of work, or whether or not he bores you to death on weekends. Nobody seems to care whether or not life with this financial genius is bearable. Nobody knows about his personality and if it is compatible with family happiness. Today, we actively breed egotism—and a lot of lonely old people as a result.

Another thing people who don't want to be alone have to learn is to stop announcing at every suitable and unsuitable occasion that the world is coming to an end. Be-

137

cause *they* have most of their life behind them and because *they* are afraid of dying, they try to make those around them suffer. In their opinion, everything, from the weather to newborn infants, is getting worse. They tell you non-stop that they don't want to have anything more to do with this rotten world, that there's nothing today except chaos, that they simply can't stand by and watch how the authority of the church, the state, the school, the father or of men in general, is being destroyed; the stupid psychologists with their mad ideas can only bring about more misery; modern music is rubbish; artists are all crazy . . . and so on and so forth.

Coupled with this bad habit, which quickly drives away even the most patient listener, is a disposition to cling stubbornly to the negative, to see only the disadvantages in everything and everybody, and to keep harping on this in every conversation.

If it's a sunny day, then, "It will be so hot in the city, we won't be able to breathe." When it rains, "This terrible weather is more than one can bear." If a grandchild shines in math, they're upset about his English. If the grandson has a girlfriend, they worry that she might be a bad influence on him. If he doesn't have a girlfriend—horrors! Is he becoming a homosexual?

Sooner or later, most people will stay away—out of pure self-defense. And nobody can blame them for it.

In Europe there seem to be fewer lonely old people than in the U.S. In Europe, families, particularly in the Mediterranean countries, are much closer. It's true that the divorce rate isn't much different in the Old World than in the New, but love between parents and children seems to be more genuine.

For example, there simply are no jokes about neurotic mothers in Europe. I remember reading an interview with social critic Fran Lebowitz in an American journal; she talked about stress and how it helps to keep your weight down. I'm thinking about a particular remark she made, swearing that you could eat tons for breakfast—bacon and eggs, toast and rolls, even cream and sugar in your coffee—and that it would not make you fat—as long as you called your mother first.

To us, this was not very funny. Most people who read the interview didn't even know where the humor was, because nagging mothers who fit this description are very rare in Europe. Of course, European mothers too have their problems. But they take good care not to burden their children with them. On the contrary, they go out of their way to make life easy for their offsprings and as a result, they are respected and deeply loved.

In Europe people enjoy visiting their parents. They do not do it out of duty. On the contrary we see them as often as possible, sometimes even go on vacations with them—and it's fun! I am not talking about myself and my own mother, but generally. I know many people who go yachting or skiing with their parents, who take them out to dinner and invite them home when entertaining their friends. Here, it is considered an honor to be introduced to someone's mother or father. It does not happen that often and, when it does it means that finally you belong to the inner circle of family friends.

European parents are great! They do not think they are worth less because they are older. On the contrary, they know that the whole family can profit from their wisdom and they possess a natural authority everyone respects. You yourself want to be like them when you grow old. And because you love them and respect them, you do not move thousands of miles away from them. Result: fewer lonely elderly people.

139

In Europe it is still the norm for young people to live at home until they get married, and for them to stay with their parents as long as they are still in school, if they live in a university town. In Europe, a twenty-two-year-old who still lives at home is not considered in anyway strange or unusual. To turn children of twenty out of the house, to let them sink or swim on their own, seems very cruel to us. It can of course be advantageous under certain circumstances. But frequently children are sent away much too early. The consequence is often rootless, neurotic people who are prone to severe depression. The eagerness for drugs, alcohol, and sometimes even violence is probably nothing more than the search for love and security.

People and trees have much in common. The longer they are cared for, protected, and pampered in their early lives, the stronger they will be and the longer they will last.

Parents who forget this shouldn't be surprised when they are deserted by their offspring and left alone in their old age. Parents who complain about ungrateful children must not forget that it was they who raised them. Any mother left high and dry by a child at the first opportunity will have to examine her conscience first. The old saying, "Youth belongs to youth," is correct only up to a point. Certainly it is important to let youngsters play with children their own age in order to amuse themselves, to let off steam. Intellectually, however, children can only profit from much older people. Even at the age of twenty-one, they still need a lot of guidance. Parents who make the effort to stand by their children as long as they live will never be lonely!

We live in materialistic times and are accustomed to investing our money and our feelings only where we are sure to get a return. Different rules, however, govern the parent-child relationship. Bringing up children is tough. Here, the investment is all one-sided. It is made by only one party, the parent(s). Parents have the duty to raise their children without regard for their own profit. Those who don't believe it will have to count on many a hard blow later on.

The importance of a mother's being strong and experienced cannot be emphasized enough. Even if she has many problems herself, it is her duty by nature to protect her children and not the other way around. Mothers who burden their young with their own problems pave the way for a very lonely old age. So do women who, abandoned by their men, raise their sons to be substitute husbands. The same goes for fathers who insist that their sons become overnight millionaires or heroes. The strain on the child is usually too much. He cannot but fail, is overcome by guilt, and in the end tries to get away as fast and as far as possible. People who are not strong enough to have children for the children's own sake should perhaps forget about having them at all and direct their time and energies elsewhere.

Parents who do not want to be left alone by their children in old age must remember the following: The best way to hang on to those kids is not to hang on at all. Mothers must stop weighing down their children with guilt feelings. It was in the United States when I heard for the first time in my life a mother say to her daughter (who wanted to go skiing over the weekend), "You go off and *what about me?*" As if the daughter were responsible for keeping her mother entertained. Never in Europe have I met with this kind of attitude. *"And what about me?"* is a sentence that was never pronounced in my home, neither by my mother nor by my father nor by me, because I can

141

look after myself, thank you. I heard a lot of other comments though: "Go ahead, and do what you have to do."
"Don't worry about me, I'm fine." "You have to live your
life. Don't let me hold you back." If seeing my mother had
made me feel guilty, if talking to her on the telephone had
made me uneasy because of her constant nagging, I would
certainly not be as close to her as I am—and she would
be a very lonely old lady now.

Many people say that loneliness in old age depends to a
great extent on one's health. As long as you're hale and
hearty, you'll have no problems. But what about when you
get sick? Well, health is not synonymous with youth. A lot
of young people have health problems too, and being sick
is never pleasant, no matter whether you're old or young.
Nobody today would question the idea that good health is
connected closely to willpower. We can do much to keep
in top shape if we decide we're simply not going to be
sick. If you want to stay healthy badly enough, you can
survive operations and accidents, no matter what your age.

My Aunt Anna was eighty-five when she fell and broke
her right hip. While she was bedridden, the family doctor
tried to prepare the family that she was about to pay her
debt to nature. He told them she probably wouldn't recover, that it was the beginning of the end, that she'd most
likely be gone before the month was up.

Six weeks later, my mother paid Aunt Anna a surprise
visit. But she wasn't in her bed and she wasn't in the living room. Finally my mother discovered the supposedly
deathly ill patient out on the balcony. The tiny white-haired
old lady was lying happily in the sun, completely naked,
doing her exercises. The doctor never forgave her for not
dying then. He became so insufferable that, at the age of
eighty-six, Aunt Anna had to look for a new physician, one

with due respect for her will to live. In fact, barely three months after her accident, she was again riding her bicycle around the city. She lived to be ninety-three, in large part because of her strong will to survive.

If you want to be healthy in old age, stop giving in to self-pity. My mother had a serious operation when she was seventy-three. The operation was a success, but the incision wouldn't heal. They had used a supposedly absorbable thread to sew up the wound, but the body rejected it. For months my mother had to wear a bandage. Finally, as nothing else worked, the doctors decided to operate again. This meant more anesthesia and another stay in the hospital.

My mother would have had good reason to give in to the same self-pity so many other older people are prone to. But not her. Never! When I called, very concerned, it was she who cheered me up. Before the first operation, when she was seriously ill, she told me, "Don't worry, it's all right."

When I took her home from the hospital, she had lost quite a bit of weight. She was as thin as a schoolgirl and unsteady on her feet. On her first evening out of the hospital, however, she insisted on going to a concert because her grandson, a member of the Vienna Boys Choir, was performing that night and had a solo. I'll never forget how she pulled herself up those stairs—the only tickets we could get were in the third balcony. Each step was terribly painful, but she made it and even managed to go backstage after the performance to congratulate her darling. It took her two days to recover from this exertion, but she has never regretted it.

Many older people make the mistake of looking at themselves much too critically. Suddenly they have time on their hands and, instead of doing interesting things for

143

which they never had time during their working years, they become introverted and keep looking for signs of illness.

Nothing is more detrimental to good health. If you sit around waiting for sickness to strike, it certainly will. The person who runs from one doctor to another, and then does the same thing all over again six months later, finally ends up thinking about nothing but doctors, clinics, and symptoms. That's certainly not the way to strengthen the body's defenses. When you live in constant fear of a certain illness, you'll soon get the first telling symptoms if you look hard enough. On the other hand, people who are too busy to worry about illness usually stay healthy.

Life can be so full of exciting discoveries. I began my college studies when I was already twenty-eight, and new dimensions opened up in the truest sense of the word. Once I had started researching English women novelists of the eighteenth century, I wanted to do nothing else. I read absolutely everything I could lay my hands on: the diaries of these fascinating women, their letters to women friends, husbands, or lovers. I was spellbound by what I learned about the ways they lived: They would spend seven hours having their hair done before a festival ball; a young lady from a well-to-do family didn't buckle her own shoes; diligent ladies' maids were able to save enough to open small shops in London that soon became the most fashionable boutiques of the day. Things we don't think about twice, items and conveniences we take for granted, were often difficult to come by. Good, white paper, for example, was very expensive, and many of the ladies who wrote novels secretly used scraps of coarse wrapping paper stolen from the kitchen when the housekeeper's back was turned.

I read newspapers and sermons of the time, as well as history books. I came to understand the causes of the In-

144

dustrial Revolution and found out about the indignation of the townspeople who, visiting a factory for the first time, were shocked to see that a worker was allowed to turn out only half an item, not a finished one. I read their prophecies about how this kind of work would affect their minds. I read the works of women writers in Paris who had been enthusiastic early supporters of the French Revolution and found out how quickly they longed for their accustomed security in England.

I read American newspapers, too, studying the ads of the time—even two hundred years ago there were ads. I was amused to learn that Philadelphia, an industrial center today, was then only a small market town, and that half of the want ads were about strayed oxen and cattle.

In short, studying changed my life. Had I had my own private fortune, or had I been a retired lady with lots of time on my hands, I would still be sitting in the reading rooms of libraries, enjoying myself more than ever.

There is so much to learn and explore in life, not only in literature or history. You can start where you want, studying tablecloths or the galaxies. There are so many secrets in the world of animals and plants that we can delve into when we're not forced to work for a living. There are arts and crafts we can learn no matter how old we are. We can make music, paint, do needlework, weave, turn our garden plot into a real garden, an oasis of peace and quiet, one that consists not merely of a lawn and three birch trees but of arbors and rose bushes, flowering shrubs and paths lined with green hedges.

The joy of being creative surpasses all expectations. The enthusiasm that grips you when you suddenly understand why plants, animals, and people behave one way and not another is overwhelming. There are so many fields of knowledge one can investigate. In every large city there are public libraries and museums. Why shouldn't we spend a couple of hours a day, just like a student, sitting in a lecture hall and finding out about the complicated love life of the salmon, or why the aborigines of New Guinea ate their own ancestors?

It doesn't matter what area you finally decide on. Surely everyone can remember some subject of childhood fascination that one had to abandon for career reasons. Take it up again. Right now! And you'll grow into a different person. If you start to study, you'll be rewarded with a fascinating glimpse into the mysteries of creation. You'll begin to understand how marvelous this world is, how many secrets there are left to plumb.

You'll also understand how relatively insignificant we all are, how absurd it is, in this universe of great splendor, to take only ourselves and our headaches seriously. Stop ignoring the world around you because of some real or imagined pain in your joints!

While thinking about our relative smallness, you'll also learn something else: the insignificance of one's own death. To be afraid of dying is useless. To spoil the last twenty years of your life because of it is downright silly. We knew right from the start that we wouldn't live forever. What good does it do to object violently to a rule of the game, a game we can't change anyway? Let's face it. We are nothing but pawns—but let's at least be happy ones.

I think it is good that we don't live forever. If you live a full life, you'll be grateful for a rest. Haven't you ever longed for genuine peace? I have, often enough. I know that one day it will be mine, and the thought does not frighten me. The idea of peace should also be of comfort to those who neither believe in God nor in an afterlife.

I am a true believer in the existence of the soul, and I

146

know that it is the soul that counts and not the body. I also believe in God because I feel His presence particularly in moments of great despair. God has never let me down throughout my entire life. I believe in Him, I need Him, and I love Him. He gives me great strength. Try and reach out to Him; you too might perceive that He is there. And, believe me, it makes life so much easier.

When my mother was waiting to have her operation, I was desperate. On the day of her surgery I got up at four in the morning, went to church, and began to pour out my heart to God. I also found a book with old church hymns, read texts I hadn't seen for years. They were very ancient and purely lyrical—"O Savior in Our Need," "Thou Refuge of the Ill"—and suddenly these words had meaning. After several hours in this beautiful Gothic church, a wave of relief came over me, and I knew that my mother was safe.

Since none of us will live forever, why not be brave and accept death as the last, fascinating episode of life? My grandmother lived in a small Austrian village and was very good friends with the local doctor. He lived to be nearly a hundred years old, and he was a sort of father and mother figure to the entire community, as he had brought several generations into the world and had taken good care of them throughout their lives. Every Sunday the frisky old man could be seen sitting at the local inn. He was inevitably in high spirits, told a good story, and as long as he could eat his Sunday lunch of boiled beef (*Tafelspitz*) with two side vegetables, all was right with the world.

Several years ago, I went back to the village. It was a Sunday and so I went to the inn. The doctor wasn't there. He had died some time before, I learned. But not in trepidation! On the contrary, he had gathered his big family

147

around his bed and told them quite matter-of-factly, as if he were giving a medical lecture, just what was going on in his body, which of his organs had ceased to function properly, and how long his heart would hold out. He refused all sedatives. "I wouldn't dream of it," he protested. "I have seen so many people die, now I finally want to know what it's really like." He was fully conscious to the last, completely composed and fearless, interested only in learning the secret that had puzzled him all his life.

While my mother was in the hospital, she had a curious experience. Whether it was during or after her operation, she's not quite sure, but she was deeply anesthetized and suddenly she saw on the wall a green box with two white stockings hanging from it. *Aha,* she thought, *If I have to die, I have to put on these stockings first.* She was neither shocked nor startled. She simply knew that these stockings were waiting for her in case this was the end of her earthly life. She didn't tell us about this until much later, when she knew she would recover. And even now when we talk about death there's never a trace of panic. Even before her operation, my mother had felt essentially the same about death. She was already in the hospital and had a very serious blood condition. "Do you know," she said, "to die of this kind of anemia is marvelous? You get pleasantly tired and long only for sleep and peace."

If you are lucky enough to be surrounded by people who accept the end of life just as they accept the beginning, then it is easy to find death fascinating. Several years ago in Paris, I had just read with great enthusiasm what the English philosopher John Stuart Mill had written more than a century ago about the inequalities of the marriage laws and about women's suffrage. Finally I buried myself in a book about his life and came upon the following sentence: "His wife Harriet Taylor, with whom he had worked closely, died of tuberculosis after only seven years of marriage in Avignon."

I had hardly finished reading the sentence when I realized I hadn't the slightest idea just how one dies of tuberculosis. You read hundreds of times that somebody has grown ill and died, but how it comes about is a puzzle. The only thing I could think of was that, during my boarding-school days, I had once made a superhuman effort to bring on a low fever so I could miss a Latin class I had not prepared for. Looking at it that way, it seemed that dying, actually ceasing to breathe, was a mighty accomplishment.

It was with great respect that I suddenly thought of my ancestors, all of whom had died successfully. Compared to them, my inability to induce even a small defect seemed to me an immense failure. *How does one do that?* I thought. *Can it be learned? How does one make one's circulation simply stop?* I hadn't the slightest idea, and for days I went around admiring all of those who had successfully switched from this life to the next.

Everything that has to do with death and what comes afterward has always filled me with the greatest curiosity. I am convinced that when my life on earth is over, I will find out a number of things: what life was all about; what order the earth, the Milky Way, and the universe all obey. That there is a fundamental law I have never doubted. I have never been presumptuous enough to think that the entire universe revolved only around me and the rest of humankind. Ants, who build their complicated, highly structured colonies, could by the same reckoning believe that they are the alpha and omega of creation.

Even though we are in a position to dirty, exploit, and even to destroy part of our planet, we are still only a tiny link in the chain of evolution, whose totality we will never be able to grasp here on earth. Despite this, life does have meaning. I know that I have my part to play and that it is not at all a matter of indifference whether I perform it well or badly.

Lord Halifax was an English statesman and moralist who lived three hundred years ago. The tone of his writings got on my nerves terribly, especially when coupled with what he had to say in his booklet on female conduct called "The Lady's New Year's Gift; or, Advice to a Daughter," which he published in 1696. He tells his child that in all probability the husband he would choose for her would make her miserable. Husbands either drink, keep mistresses, or gamble. They are either very stupid or mean with money. If they are bright, they will be ill-tempered, and there is no way out, he tells his beloved child. Since women have to marry, they will have to cope with husbands the way they are.

This, of course, annoyed me. However, he did write a few good lines about life and death, and they are appropriate to this discussion. He tells his daughter that life was worth living if she kept her faith in God and trusted in His goodness and benevolence. The secret of a happy life, he finally tells her, lies in the acquisition "of such a wise resignation that you may live in the world *so as it may hang about you like a loose garment, and not tied too close to you.*" And this, to my mind, is very sound advice indeed.

But let's get back to our own century. If you are scared of growing old, start a collection. Not of books or stamps but of people who have managed to overcome their apprehensions or, better still, who have never known any in the first place. You can call them or write to them whenever you're in trouble, but usually it's enough to *know* that they're there, and already you start to feel better. I have been collecting such people for a long time, at home and abroad, men and women—and the older they are, the better they have served my purpose.

One of my latest conquests is a lovely American lady, named Helen. She is nowhere near being old. When I first met her, she was barely sixty. But she has intrigued me because she belongs to a social class where, especially in America, you do not find very many women who radiate energy and joy. I am talking about the wives of very rich men.

Helen is short, with a nice, firm body. She has a lovely face and keeps her hair tied carelessly back. She wears pants and sweaters in which she feels good and, if she *has* to look elegant, well, she can manage that too.

Her husband is one of the nicest rich men I have ever met. He has made every penny himself without shortcuts or hurting anyone. He loves his wife, his children and grandchildren, and still leads an active business life. With three partners, he has acquired a small château in France complete with vineyards and a wine cellar, not far from Bordeaux. Three months a year the castle is his, and before they go down there they usually stop over in Paris. That's how I met them.

I first set eyes on Helen at a party at a fashionable Parisian apartment. The food was excellent, the conversation excruciatingly dull. Everybody stood around, glass in hand, looking sophisticated. The elegant ladies sported their special expression, something between pained and pampered, which must have something to do with being married to the very wealthy. Anyway, in the middle of all this there was Helen.

Helen did not talk in a blasé voice about the rising dollar or the plummeting French franc. Neither did she look discreetly at her watch to see whether or not she could safely leave. She stood there, hand on hip, talking with great animation about a nice, old French lady sporting a scarf and shopping basket, whom she had observed earlier in the day at a street market. "I have been looking for this woman for over a year," she explained. "I am a sculptor. As soon as I get back to Florida, I am going to model her in clay, and then we'll see. Maybe I'll do her in bronze. But before that, as you all know, I'm going to be mistress of a castle for three months. Not bad, is it? But I take it as it comes. Afterward, I am good old Helen again. And that's all right too."

At the mere thought of Helen, I'm in a good mood. She is so full of life and always ready to boost your spirits. She considers her age an asset. She is proud to be a grand-mother *and* good-looking. Her age couldn't bother her less. What is it but numbers on a piece of paper? She is not "a sixty-year-old." She is Helen. She is above the abstract fig-ure. She is, will always be, herself: well-balanced, opti-mistic, with a flair for the beautiful, and a gift for making those around her happy.

Helen is never bored. I spent two weekends with her at the château. We took long walks and always found count-less topics of conversation. Time raced by in her presence. She talked about her life, of the money problems she had known as a newlywed in New York, of her conviction that she had married the right man, and of her children. "I am happy things are going well for us now," she said, "but I've also had my fill of bad times. Believe me, if I had to, I could survive without money. What comes, comes. And with God's help, we'll be all right."

As soon as the children were grown, Helen and her husband moved to Florida. Was she lonely? Not at all. She began to sculpt, took courses, and opened a small gallery. She sells only to private clients, but she has talent and works with great enthusiasm. She spends several days a month in New York, going to museums and galleries. She doesn't miss a single exhibition. Spends as much time as she can with her grandchildren. "I'm never lonely for a second," she emphasizes, "but I have never felt bored in my whole life. Wherever I look there are so many things to do and learn. This will undoubtedly still be the case even when I'm eighty." The little old Parisian who made such an impression on her at the market has long since been immortalized in metal. She was the star attraction of Helen's most recent exhibition.

Anybody who has an open mind, a warm personality, and a talent for seeing the positive side of life will have no trouble fascinating young people. Another member of my collection is Birgit Martens from Austria. We first met on the *Orient Express* between Paris and Vienna. Birgit had just turned seventy and I was thirty-three. We hit it off right away and kept up the conversation throughout the entire trip. When we arrived in Vienna we agreed to stay in touch. We exchanged addresses, and I promised to call her the next time I was back home. Two years elapsed.

This first meeting came at an unbelievably hectic time for me. I had finished my studies, had moved from France to Austria, and started my career as a journalist. For my first two years in Vienna, I worked nearly day and night. Even on weekends I was usually busy, hot on the trail of some interesting story for the paper, writing articles, planning books. For two days and nearly one whole night I sat in the Hotel Imperial in Vienna trying to convince the queen of Spain to grant me an interview, her first ever. I fought numerous battles with bodyguards and secretaries in order to get an interview with the Saudi Arabian oil minister Sheik Ahmed Zaki Yamani. I was working at full tilt. There was no time left over to call old acquaintances or even to lead a private life. But enough is enough. Just as I had decided to slow down, to see some friends and keep the weekends to myself, I got a telephone call. It was Birgit Martens.

"Recently I read an article in the paper about colors," she said, "and I knew only you could have written it." She had called me at the newspaper office, taking potluck, as I had neither told her that I was back in town nor given her my new address. I was so happy to hear from her that we met that very evening and chatted until one o'clock in the morning.

Since then, we've met at regular intervals. In the summer we sit on the terrace of my favorite café, right next to City Hall Park. In the winter we take turns visiting one another. Not long ago we were talking about the advantages and disadvantages of our respective ages, and I listened intently as she said, "The greatest problem of my age is being alone."

When I asked her what she did all day, she told me the following: She got up early, did her housework, answered her mail, and went shopping. After this she started to cook since her granddaughter ate lunch with her every noon. After lunch she washed the dishes and then indulged in a few quiet hours during which she did needlework. When asked to specify, it turned out that she created marvelous wall hangings and restored rare antique rugs.

For four hours each day, usually between four in the afternoon and eight at night, she took care of her dying daughter-in-law. When she finally came home, she ate supper with an American art student to whom she had rented a room. In between, she still found time to transcribe old family documents and letters, which were written in the old Gothic script, to make them accessible to her children and grandchildren. In addition, she took care of a large house just outside of Vienna that had belonged to her grandparents. She tended the garden, chopped wood, tied up the rosebushes, planted flower bulbs, and cooked for her three children and their children, particularly on summer weekends when they fled the city to breathe some clean air in the country.

"How can you say you're lonely?" I asked in astonishment. "There are loads of young people who don't do half the things you do."

Birgit thought a minute. "Perhaps lonely is not the right word," she said. "When I reconsider, it isn't really loneliness. It is more the feeling of uselessness." With all the work she does! Hadn't she ever realized it would cost her family a small fortune if they had to hire somebody to cook, clean, and nurse for them, not to mention all the other work she does?

No, she hadn't. What she had done was something else. She had compared her life today with the life she had led as a young woman when, after her husband's sudden death in the closing days of World War II, she was left to care for their three small children. In those chaotic times the life or death of the family had depended solely on her. There was barely any food, and no milk. In Vienna, infants died by the thousands. There was virtually no public assistance. Widows' pensions and social security payments were too meager to meet the needs. The government was about to collapse, and women were scared to death of the occupying armies, in particular the first wave of invading Russian troops.

Birgit was alone and had only herself to count on, but she saw it through. She proved that she was a winner. As a young girl she had learned dressmaking and weaving. She began to look for customers and to sew dresses. She worked around the clock in unheated rooms with inadequate lighting. Slowly, things got better. She had her regular clients. She was able to send the children to good schools, and they all went on to college, although there were no scholarships at that time. All three did well. One daughter is the assistant director of a large firm, the other a writer. The son manages a law office.

Compared to that period, Birgit says, her existence today is commonplace. I told her she was so wrong! How can anyone compare a time of utter chaos, a time of crisis brought on by a lost war, to a period of general well-being? Nobody is starving in Austria today. If all parents found life worthwhile only in the struggle for survival, in the endeavor to keep their children from starving to death, they could collectively throw themselves out of their windows as utterly useless human beings.

Birgit Martens is making a mistake typical of many industrious women. She judges herself too harshly, others too leniently. Her main problem is her own modesty. There is no question that she is needed, that she is the mainstay of her family. If she would only stand still for a minute, she'd see this too, but she doesn't. She is not aware of her own worth. She doesn't waste time converting her work into money, calculating how much she is saving her family. In spite of her intelligence, she has become a victim of the old-age terror of our time.

Because she was told that older people were in trouble, she began to invent problems, to identify with people with whom she has absolutely nothing in common. That's the reason she complained of her "lonely old age," although it was evident after only two minutes of conversation that this did not apply to her at all.

Just a little bit of praise from her family would have freed Birgit from all these doubts. But children are often ungrateful and very slow to acknowledge somebody else's contributions. Sometimes children have to bump into things with their noses before they appreciate just what they have. Too often they realize how much their father, mother, or grandmother meant to them only after they've lost them.

It would work wonders if, now and then, we took a few minutes to look at the daily contributions of the elderly and—since money has all but replaced God in our society—consider what their efforts would have cost if we had had to hire somebody else to do this work.

If you don't consider housework work, then consider what a good conversational partner is worth, a person who is in a position to listen and advise. We all know what a psychiatrist charges per hour. A wise and older member of the family, on the other hand, "costs" nothing. Just what is his or her presence worth? A person you can trust absolutely, someone who has already experienced and accomplished much, a member of your own family who is not going to be jealous of your success and will therefore help you as much as he or she possibly can?

Older people can enrich our lives, and all sensible people value what they have to say. A well-known Viennese interior decorator who has so many commissions he doesn't know what to do first always has time for one thing: his evening of cards with a group of pensioners in one of those comfortable Viennese coffeehouses. "They know what life is all about," he says, "and when they talk I keep my mouth shut. I don't learn in a week what I learn from my pensioners in one single evening."

The world needs the experience of the older people— today more than ever. Age has been respected in all of the great culture of bygone years, and we are slowly beginning to discover its worth anew. But older people also have to help themselves. They must not stoop too low: He who bows too low will be stepped on. Stop the false modesty! If Birgit Martens had not taken the initiative on the *Orient Express*, we would both have lost much. She might have been tempted to think, *This woman is nearly forty years younger than I. What have I to offer her?* Thank heavens she didn't do that, and we are both richer as a result.

So far we have discussed "lonely old age" only in relation to women with children. What about those women who never married and have no family? Don't they have even more to fear? Not necessarily. The best example I know of is an unbeatable old lady named Lisa Feldner. My father was an orchestra conductor, and she was his last pianist. When she talks about her life, you want her to go on and on and never stop.

She was born in 1896. Her parents sent her to boarding school, and it was there that she studied music and learned to play the piano. And what did she do when she graduated? She became a member of an elegant all-woman orchestra and toured the world. She traveled throughout Europe as well as Egypt, Morocco, and Tunisia. She played in the grand concert cafés of those times and had more admirers than she could handle.

She gave in once: She married a musician but divorced him two years later. In order to forget her marriage, she learned to play another instrument, the trumpet, and soon signed up for more concert tours.

She happened to be in Europe just as my father was looking for a pianist. She wrote him a short letter, the shortest job application he had ever received. She didn't even include her birth date. In ten days, she wrote, she would come to the house for an audition. And come she did. My father's first thought was, *Well, she's certainly no spring chicken,* and he was right—she was not beautiful either, wearing an old gray-green coat and an indefinable hat. What was most striking was her big nose.

Then she sat down at the piano and began to play. My father smiled and began putting one piece of music after another in front of her nose. She played everything he gave her, sight-reading those pieces she did not know, and then the miracle happened; my father fetched his violin, and, to the delight of us all, the two of them played duets for the rest of the afternoon until well into dinnertime. He hired her on the spot, and she stayed with him until he died six years later.

If Lisa Feldner had written the usual letter of application, he probably wouldn't even have wanted to see her. When she came to us, she was already seventy-three! Luckily, she did not care. On stage, and in an elegant long dress, she made a striking figure, and her playing was excellent. Her greatest asset was her total lack of false modesty. Lisa plays even today, and she'll continue to play until the day she drops dead at the base of her piano at the age of a hundred or more. She works constantly. In the summer she plays with an orchestra at a health spa. In the winter she plays at an elegant concert café in Vienna. During the few weeks between engagements, she travels around the world and visits her friends.

As I said, we didn't meet her until she was over seventy—and there's an old saying that you don't make real friends in your later years. Well, it's not true. Lisa Feldner has become a very dear friend of the family. She visits us, we visit her, and we aren't the only people with whom she remains in close contact. Last year she even fell in love again. Lisa can't complain of being lonely, that's for sure.

One more word about appearances, to get it out of the way: There are marvelously beautiful old people, men as well as women. Most of them were also beautiful and attractive in their youth. But many others became so only in their later years, through their experience and the personality they have acquired by working on themselves. It is poise, kindness, dignity, and the facial expressions that we find beautiful. Wrinkles don't diminish that. This kind of beauty has more substance. For this reason, beautiful old people leave a more lasting impression than the beautiful young.

I still remember an elegant English gentleman I met during my first year in England. It was summer, and, as I often did on weekends, I had gone to see my former husband's grandmother at her house in Brighton. Grandmama had a big mansion and rented various floors to summer guests. She had let the top floor to this particular man and his wife.

The first time I saw him I was speechless. I was standing at the window with a cup of tea in my hand, watching this tall, slender, and imposing man cross the garden to the street. He had a noble face and a shock of white hair. I found out from Grandmama he had been a colonial officer in India. She also added that he was eighty-six years old. I almost dropped the teacup. I couldn't believe it. The impression he made on me, a young woman barely twenty-five, was so great, I can still see his face before me even today.

There's a lot to tell about Grandmama as well. The moment I met her I said to myself, *Aha, this is a real lady*. (She reminded me right away of an old friend of the family, whom I called Aunt Clara. Aunt Clara was the epitome of the elegant lady and a real woman of the world. When I was sixteen she told me, "Remember this: The most important thing in life is to become a lady. That takes time. But once you've done it, you'll stay beautiful until you die.

160

Ladies never grow old." She herself proved this sufficiently.)

But back to my English grandmama. She was a real lady, although her life had been difficult and there was a certain hardness about her you couldn't overlook. She came from a good family and wanted to be a painter. She studied for a while and, when she married, she received a big dowry. At first she painted, but not for long. She soon found that her husband was rapidly squandering their joint fortune through neglect and ineptitude. She took things into her own hands and managed, just barely, to save the two houses she had brought to the marriage.

I met Grandmama when she was eighty-three. She was not exactly a lovable person, but one had to respect her. The family accepted her as the strongest member of the clan, and everybody took her seriously. She lived alone in one of the two houses she owned, and never even considered going into a nursing home. She enjoyed her home and garden; she painted many afternoons; she cooked every day because she enjoyed it. During the week she baked her own bread and, on Sundays, marvelous little cakes, "rock cakes," made with unbleached flour and lots of raisins. She took no medication but swore by the vitamin B preparation called brewer's yeast. She took it daily. "My dear child," she said to me, "you must remember one thing: There's no secret to living a long life. You can do everything, absolutely everything. But you have to do it with style and in moderation."

When I first saw Grandmama she was sitting in an elegant armchair in my mother-in-law's house; her hair was attractively combed, her cheeks lightly rouged, her lips delicately tinted. She was the best proof that nothing is more complimentary to an older woman than a little bit of color in her face. In France they have known for years

161

that delicately rouged cheeks are an ideal contrast to white hair. And if you, like Grandmama at the age of eighty-three, also have a beautiful mouth, why should you not emphasize it?

The more usual approach—"Now I'm old, so I shouldn't really pretty myself up"—is pure poppycock. Old or young, you are always the same person. I saw pictures of Grandmama as a young girl. She has the same high forehead and big clear eyes now. Why should she have stopped taking care of herself?

Well-groomed older women who are so attractive that you often turn around to look at them on the street are quite a common sight in Italy and in France. During my first year in Paris I met one of them. A doctor's family had invited me to spend two weeks with them in the country, in a beautiful, old, gray stone house in Brittany.

The house belonged to Grandmère. She had turned eighty that summer. She had a long-haired dachshund, and her inexhaustible humor and energy made her one of the most lovable people I have ever met. Although the family had daughters my age, I preferred to spend my time with her. She was an interesting personality. She wasn't beautiful in the classical sense because she was a bit too plump (she loved good food). But she had such a radiance about her and a certain bounce in her movements that she created a stir, even on a crowded street.

I spent marvelous days with Madame Bralé. The weather was gorgeous and, in the morning, we sat together in the garden, under a giant linden tree, shelling peas or snapping green beans while a village girl did the more unpleasant tasks of cutting up onions and peeling potatoes. The dog lay at our feet, the bees buzzed, and for hours we talked about wartime France, about her youth, her happy marriage, the lives of Chopin and Mozart (Madame Bralé was an excellent pianist), and whether or not the French concert piano Gaveau could match the Austrian Bösendorfer.

Madame Bralé's philosophy was simple. It consisted of one sentence: Life was beautiful! She was an outspoken optimist and managed to see everything in a positive light. She had loved her husband very much and, instead of lamenting the fact that she had been a widow for seven years, she took pleasure in remembering how happy her thirty years of married life had been. "Suzanne," she said to me, "you have to get married. I was married for thirty years, and for thirty years I was happy." It seemed she spoke the truth because she had not a trace of bitterness about her whole being.

Madame took seriously whatever she did, her midday meal as well as her wardrobe. Every day after lunch and coffee, at about two-thirty in the afternoon, she took a kettle of hot water up to her bedroom (there was no running water in the house, only a cistern). As she climbed the steps to the second floor, she announced to us all: *"Mes enfants, je monte faire ma toilette"* ("My children, I am going upstairs to freshen up").

And when she reappeared at about five o'clock, she wore a pretty dress, a bit of rouge and lipstick, and a silk scarf that went with her outfit; she carried a book or piano music under her arm, and the dog followed behind. She was a very pleasant sight. Best of all, there was an air of contentment about her and the feeling that all was right with the world. And even though one knows that this isn't the case, it is very nice to give in to the illusion and enjoy a few peaceful hours as a result.

Youth has no monopoly on good grooming and an interest in clothes. If you have a good figure and you like to dress up, you should wear what you like. The nasty accusation, "Your clothes are too young for you," words that disturbed generations of women, are seldom heard in this day and age. What these people really meant was something else: "You look much too young and how dare you emphasize it." Today there's only one guide—your own taste. Nobody is going to be forced to dress as they did in the nineteenth century. If you're the sporty kind, what's wrong with blue jeans and a simple pullover? Even when you're eighty you can still show off your figure in a bathing suit. There's no reason an elegant older woman can't show off her good points just as she did when she was young. And this brings us back to Aunt Clara.

Aunt Clara was the epitome of the elegant Viennese lady. She was tall, blonde, busty, and full of life. When she traveled, and she did so even at the age of ninety, it was always with four hatboxes. She is dead now, unfortunately, but she lived to be eighty-nine, and she never lost any of her fascination. Every year of her life she spent her summer vacation in the country, in my grandmother's village. There was always much excitement just before her arrival. The rooms were aired out, the bedding changed, flowers were gathered for bouquets, and rugs were beaten. Then she would appear in her traveling outfit and silk scarf, smelling wonderful, accompanied by numerous pigskin suitcases and the inevitable hatboxes, which for me were a symbol of the elegant world.

She stayed in the most beautiful house in the village. It was right next to the church and had been built as the summer residence of the bishops of Passau. Her apartment consisted of three rooms outfitted with dark, heavy furniture and marvelous rugs in glowing colors. There was also a glass-fronted cabinet with fascinating objects inside, among them a crystal smelling-salts bottle and a container for attar of roses.

She had visiting hours every afternoon, and I used to knock shyly and stand, with my heart pounding fiercely, in front of the high, heavy, polished oak door, waiting for the marvelously trilled, *"Herrein!"* ("Come in!"). I would have preferred to spend whole days in her presence. That's how great the attraction of this older lady was for me the child. Nobody, but nobody, would have dreamed of making fun of her clothes, scarves, hats, or costly perfumes.

Growing old can be beautiful, a blessing. Do it properly and you have nothing to fear. No false sense of modesty and no giving in. Head high, show what kind of wood you're carved from. Life is so thrilling; there's so much to do. The secret recipe is to grow old in style, with courage and humor. There are plenty of examples for us to follow, and no reason in the world we shouldn't succeed.

7

The Young Mistress— Not to Be Feared, but Pitied

Every married woman is afraid, if only in the abstract, that her husband will fall for a younger rival, the kind who turns a man's head and lures him away from home into a love nest of her own where he'll pamper and spoil her with furs and diamonds for one reason only: because she is younger than the wife.

Nothing could be further from the truth. Young women who are showered with love and presents by older admirers exist, for the most part, only in a betrayed wife's tortured brain. Right from the start, let's make one thing clear: The danger lies not in the other woman's youth but in the fact that she's different. It's the tantalizing desire for novelty that can endanger a marriage, not the wrinkles on the wife's face.

A man who has a tendency to stray from the path, whose need for a change cannot be subdued, will tire of a younger playmate much sooner than he will of a woman his own age. There's a well-known Parisian dandy who proves this time and again. He is a habitué of several restaurants and coffee shops where artists meet, and he loves to show off his newest conquests. Most of them are young American

166

students, and his interest in them wanes regularly at the end of three weeks. His only long-lived affair, according to the coffeehouse crowd, was with a woman his own age; to the astonishment of all, she lasted for ten months.

I am constantly amazed at the vast number of women who are scared to death of a younger competitor. Believe me, this is ridiculous. It's also a waste of time. You might just as well sit around waiting for the plague to strike. Fortunately, most wives will never find themselves in a situation where they are seriously threatened by a younger woman. Their fears do not spring from experience. They are, rather, roused by loose talk, silly remarks, old clichés, outdated jokes, and hackneyed phrases.

Since human beings are by nature easily frightened, they greedily absorb fears; and, once these fears are fixed in the imagination, they become stronger than life itself.

In general, the rule holds true that a younger woman cannot break up a good marriage or relationship. Men are better than we are led to believe by journalists who write in second-rate "men only" illustrated magazines. How many playboys and men about town are there anyway? You could probably count them on the fingers of both hands. You can compare these types with Mr. Average just about as easily as you can compare former Persian Empress Soraya with the woman on the street.

Every now and then, however, it does happen that a man leaves his wife and moves in with another woman, but this very seldom occurs only because she's younger. The key to the problem is the marriage itself and the question of whether or not it has become intolerable. Women will finally have to stop blaming heaven for their "bad luck." If a marriage is turning sour, it is up to them to do something about it. It doesn't matter whether you decide to go back to school, throw yourself into your job, separate, or work harder at the relationship because you feel there's something worth saving. The most important thing is to do something. If you don't, you're giving other women, including younger ones, a shot at your man.

So much has already been written about "the other woman" that we accept it as gospel. This is unfortunate because, once these images are stuck in our brains, we have a very hard time getting rid of them. In the late 1950s "the other woman" was dumb, delicate, cuddly, erotic, clinging, and young. Most recently, she has progressed in life: She is now a student; she's in research; she likes to experiment sexually; she's no longer a young child, but her hair is always long and bouncing. She's enthusiastic, hungry for admiration, and above all she's ruthless. She would step over anybody, including her own grandmother, when she sets her sights on somebody else's husband.

Whether the medium presenting such images is superficial movies, wildly unrealistic romantic novels, cheap illustrated stories, or mediocre TV programs, the wife is always innocent, at a disadvantage, and betrayed. The young rival, however, is having the time of her life and is sure of her conquest. The story has always been presented from the wife's point of view. What happened between the victorious rival and the husband later on, we were never told.

There are reasons for this. Had the screenwriters, novelists, and journalists done any research on the aftermath of the battle, it would have meant the end of their cliché woman. The sequel is often far removed from what you'd expect. The abandoned wife has no cause for despair: Neither the husband nor the young rival remains on cloud nine. Things are undoubtedly worse for the girlfriend than for the wife. Very probably, unless the wife agrees, there will never be a divorce. The other woman will end up wasting her time, and experience her first real psychological beating. In all probability she'll avoid married men in the future like the plague. She'll need at least two years to get over the trauma. The husband, on the other hand, will go back to his wife, repentant and—depending on his temperament—swearing never to stray from home and hearth again (or at least not in the immediate future).

In order to get rid of this hysterical fear of younger women, of the hatred connected with it, all you have to do is keep your eyes open and see what goes on around you. You'll have to look hard before you find a happy mistress. I know, because I wasted five years of my life in this degrading situation, and I never want to go through it again. I barely managed to survive, and that is no exaggeration. Looking back at it now with a clear head, I realize how slight the chances are that "the other woman" will end up happy. She is in a terribly difficult situation, and her biggest handicap is exactly what is feared most by the wife: her youth.

Despite the propaganda, the young woman is the weakest party in the arrangement. A novice at the game, she believes every word her married man tells her. Usually she is head over heels in love with him and convinced that his intentions are serious. She admires his superior knowledge, his self-assurance, his social status, and his financial position, which is usually greatly superior to her own. It will be eons before she is able to admit to herself that he has lied to her and had been lying right from the start.

I know of no married man who says to a young woman: "My home life is pretty good. My wife is a lovely person who gives me all the strength and security I need for my career. I love her dearly and will never leave her. All I want from you is a little excitement." Oh no. The story he tells is different. "When I am with you," he says, "I don't smoke and I don't drink too much. This means that you are very good for me. My wife drives me out of the house. She does not understand me. She never has. I'm sure she doesn't love me anymore. All I am to her is a meal ticket. But I need warmth. I need understanding. I need someone who believes in me. Lately, I have been drinking much too much. Will you help me stop? Will you stay with me?"

An experienced woman knows after the second sentence what's going on and keeps her hands off. A young one, whose ideals haven't been put to the test, believes every word and is grateful that finally a noble purpose in life has been laid before her. She is going to save this unhappy man. She is proud he has chosen her. She is going to give her very best. A lot of water will flow over the dam before she realizes she has become his victim.

It's easy to cheat young women. That's the main reason why older married men go for them. They have nothing against women their own age, except that they have become too smart. They don't believe the old story anymore. They have heard it too many times already. They refuse to get involved, or, if they do, they turn their back as soon as they find out there is no hope, that he'll never leave his wife, that she herself is just second best. The young, however, have never been hurt before. If doubts come up, they are easily persuaded that it is just a matter of time (until the mortgage is paid, the children grown up, the job promotion has come through). So they hang on and hold out, and the more it hurts the more ardently they believe that all is going to end well. It's so easy to lead a young woman around by the nose.

The second reason some older men go back to younger women is physical. Men who don't have much to give in the sexual sense often look for younger women because they are much less demanding in bed. A younger, not yet sexually mature woman longs much more for warmth, togetherness, and affection than for real sexual fulfillment. She is also thrilled to be taken to expensive restaurants that she herself would never be able to afford. Her head is turned by what she presumes is the bettering of her social position, and she regards every glass of champagne in an expensive bar as a true sign of love. If life in bed isn't all that exciting, what does it matter?

As for the man, he gains on all fronts. Within his circle of cronies, he has perpetuated the myth that the younger the woman, the hungrier she is for sexual fulfillment. He is regarded as "quite a man" although it takes considerably more to satisfy a woman of forty than a girl of twenty. He is envied because he "goes around with such a young chick." He has killed two flies with one blow: On the one hand he has acquired a sexual partner who doesn't demand much, on the other hand, a reputation among his male friends as a stud.

Older men like young women because they are easy to manipulate. They are not bored by housework yet, they happily spend time preparing candlelit dinners, and they would not dream to ask their man of the world to do the washing up. As long as the affair is young, they radiate youthful optimism, they are always in a good mood and, above all, they are tireless listeners.

Every man loves an audience. And most men like to talk. A young woman, listening with delight to what a man has to say, is unbeatable. She hangs on his every word and is fascinated by the same stories the wife has heard until she is sick—in particular, how good he is at his job. Nearly all men are insecure, even those who have made it professionally. Most men thrive on flattery; they crave admiration, no matter by whom, and young women are experts in dishing out compliments.

Of course, the search for lost youth is part of the older man–younger woman relationship. But it is often a two-edged sword, and I'll come back to this later. First a few words on self-assurance. If a man is well balanced and knows his own worth, if on top of it all he has found a woman he loves, then he will not need a mistress. On the other hand, a man who is unsure of himself, who lacks self-confidence, who believes that deep down he is—pardon me—a son of a bitch, such a man is much more apt to stray from home and get involved with other women, preparing the ground for three-fold unhappiness: His wife's, his girlfriend's, and his own.

There are many men in this world who do not see why they shouldn't hang on to more than one woman. They feel great at the thought of having two apartments to come home to. They simply are not prepared to give up anything. They want the girlfriend, but they will hang on to the wife for life. And here is where the problem starts. If this kind of man can afford two women, he'll certainly do everything in his power to keep them both. Nothing can force him to change his mind, neither the girlfriend's tears nor the wife's remonstrances. Only when he is in danger of losing both of them will he make a decision. And in ninety-nine cases out of a hundred, he'll settle for the wife.

The young woman who has successfully lured her married man away from home, or, rather, who has allowed herself to be caught in the clutches of a man with a polygamous nature, is not to be feared or hated but pitied. The poor creature has no idea what lies ahead of her. She actually thinks that she has won the battle. The man has left home and has moved in with her. Surely this is victory? It must be. The struggle to get that far was bad enough. She has to believe that the worst is behind her— for pure self-protection.

Yet, the fact that the man has moved out does not prove a thing. No final decisions have been made. The fighting is only just about to begin: over the children; over the wife's car; over time, love, attention, and of course over money. Worst of all, the fighting does not lead to the young rival's happiness. The road to divorce is long. Most men don't even dare to take the first step.

Some years ago, I lived in Paris as the mistress of a married man. He was American, twelve years older than I was, and brilliant in his career. He had been with his wife for seventeen years and had two teenage children. I loved this man to distraction. You can go back and read the effects of this affair on my health in chapter 2. But here I want to talk about something more basic.

We lived in Paris and, as likes attract likes, our circle of friends consisted mainly of well-to-do married men over forty and their young mistresses who were twenty-five or older.

To make a long story short, of all those couples only one is still together. The others have either separated or are in the process of doing so. Some had been together for ten years. One couple even had two children.

One thing I noticed right away: The stereotype of the spoiled and pampered young mistress was nowhere to be found. All the girls were miserable. They fought hard for love and recognition, suffered terribly over being number two, tried to break away at regular intervals and could never get used to the fact that weekends and part of the vacations belonged to "the family." A young woman in love with an older married man has a certain unhappy, bewildered look in her eyes, a look I can spot from a distance of ten miles. I can't bear to see it. I wore it for too long myself.

The men we're talking about are above-average wage earners. They are usually professionally powerful, but they are weak in private and unable to disentangle their love life. I call these men "O-H-H men," because they have three telephone numbers instead of two. In their business partners' address books (or their friends'), they are listed under: Office-Home-Home. The first private number is the "official" residence, where the wife and the children live. If you dial the second number you get the mistress's apartment, which is a decidedly inferior dwelling.

The family home is paid for by the salary, the other from the expense account. And here we are already confronted with the biggest obstacle to the girlfriend's aspirations of ever becoming the legal wife: Money.

There is almost never any money in the alternative household. First of all, a man has more expense with two women than with only one, and, secondly, he probably mistrusts his younger partner financially. The fascination with which she had listened to stories of his professional successes, her eagerness to hear more and more (which so charmed him at the beginning) suddenly puts him on his guard. She becomes suspect. What does she really want? Is she after his money? Is she living with him only because she thinks she can use him? If she really loves him, let her prove it. The best way to do this is by asking for nothing. She should be thankful he has taken so many inconveniences on himself for her sake. Not to mention the amount of time he gives her, costly time, stolen from his family!

The deserted wife, who often sees her budget cut in order to finance the extravagance of the new relationship, is nevertheless convinced that her rival is living in the lap of luxury. Where does the money go if not to the other woman? There are bitter fights over bank accounts, insurance premiums, and household money. The wife believes she is the only person hurt. She suffocates in self-pity and, in so doing, loses much too much of her energy. Yet, she is not the only one who suffers.

Her husband, you see, is in an even more ticklish situation. He who had impressed his young girlfriend by bragging about his position and his money is now demanding that she economize. Since he is not sure how long this relationship is going to last, he tries to get through it by spending as little money as possible. He cuts corners where he can, first of all on the rent. This again benefits his wife. The more unsightly the quarters are that he has rented for himself and his mistress, the more he longs for his accustomed and usually luxurious surroundings.

When I came to Paris and was drawn into the circle I have already described, I soon found out that the O-H-H men follow certain patterns. It was considered chic to have the family live in one of the best districts in an elegant apartment and to live with your girlfriend in a small "studio" in the student quarter. (It was also just as chic to know the owner of a certain nightclub and the first name of a certain lady bartender, but that is simply an aside.)

Should the deserted wife suffer envy and jealousy, it is only because she has no idea what the young rival has to go through. The girlfriend knows intuitively that her man will never feel comfortable in the restricted surroundings of his love nest. She knows he feels a certain ease in his bohemian role, first of all because it gives him the illusion of being a student again, and secondly because it gives him the right to say, "Look at how modestly I'm living here. Everybody can see I'm taking nothing away from my

175

family." But she senses that it can't last forever. A man who is accustomed to coming home to a six-room apartment at five o'clock in the afternoon after the office closes, taking a bath, and relaxing is not going to be happy for long with a shower in the corner of the kitchen. The wife usually has no idea that the mistress feels much more jealous than she does. It is not only the wife's influence she competes against but also everything associated with her and her supposed luxury: the larger apartment, the car, and the tennis club to which she may belong. The friend of one of my acquaintances—she was German and he was English—built a cement wall all by herself (and even took the time and trouble to paper it) in order to separate from the kitchen the entryway of the small studio she shared with her married lover. The idea was to create the illusion of a real apartment. Nothing could keep her from doing this, once she had seen with her own eyes the suits of rooms the wife occupied (the wife had gone off skiing).

The enmity with which her beloved friend reacted to her toil, reflected in remarks such as, "Every penny you spend in this dump is a total waste," should have told her how their relationship stood. But she was too young and believed him when he proclaimed, when in a good mood, "My place is with you, and I feel at home here."

The first fight between the married man and his mistress is usually over finances: for instance, when the husband doesn't give her enough money to run the household. The idyllic love that the young woman and, naturally, the man as well had hoped for is now suffocating in the mundane and the profane: one example, the problem of laundry.

There are, of course, certain married men who don't

hesitate to send their dirty laundry back to the woman they left behind (and women who are dumb enough to wash it). But in most cases the young rival has to contend with taking care of his dirty shirts, shorts, and socks. Now the problems begin. To send the wash out is expensive and too much for the household budget. To do it herself and have the kitchen full of dripping shirts when *he* comes home is impossible. So, while the wife is fighting for money to have her car repaired or to send the children to summer camp, the young mistress is struggling to find enough change to buy butter, meat, and milk—and take care of the laundry.

No man on earth is happy about handing out household money. And his dislike grows proportionally when, instead of one, suddenly *two* women are holding out their hands. Even here, as a rule, the wife comes out better. She has her regular household check, while the mistress often has to be content with the cash the man has in his pocket. Even if she's the most frugal person in the world, his astonishment is as great as his distrust when there's no more money in the kitty.

All the women who were in the same situation I was in had money problems. Most of them worked, some of them only part time, but there was not one who stayed home and let herself, as they say, be kept. All of us spent the money we earned for the household. I tried wherever I could to earn something. I was still a student, but I wrote a few articles, did some translations, and in spite of this I always had the feeling I was a parasite.

The mistress can ask for a regular allowance until her teeth drop out. The man will turn her down. Regular money is, to him, another tiresome obligation, and he has enough of those already, with respect to his wife and children. With his friend, he wants an easy and carefree relationship. The more it turns into a marriage, the more uncomfortable he feels.

In my case, the money problems took bizarre forms indeed. There were constant fights over tiny sums. My married friend insisted on eating well, and yet demanded that I purchase the groceries not in a delicatessen but at the supermarket. There is, however, a huge difference in quality between a Parisian supermarket and a *charcuterie,* where one can get fresh, homemade patés and other delicacies to which his tastebuds were accustomed. In any case, I was the loser. Either he didn't like the food or I had spent too much money. It really wasn't easy.

We even had fights about bus fare. I had to go to the library every day to do research for my dissertation. I could take either the *métro* (subway) or the bus. The bus route was beautiful. It took you along the Luxembourg Gardens, over two bridges spanning the Seine, past Notre Dame, and then, after passing the Louvre, I walked through the marvelously beautiful garden of the Palais Royal. When the weather was good I took the bus. Although the cost was minimal, this too became part of our arguments: the *métro* was half a franc cheaper.

Fights about money can kill romantic love faster than separation. This intensifies when the rival also notices that she isn't taken seriously and that the only sense of responsibility the man is capable of is directed toward his wife and children. "No matter how long you study," I was told time and again, "I'll always earn more money than you." This he followed up with an accounting of money, stocks and mortgages, of insurance policies and building-society contracts that would ensure his children and his wife a secure future. If I dared to open my mouth and ask, "And what about my future?" he became very upset. Confronting the future is usually more than the man can handle. It usually takes all his strength to muddle through the present. What he is really thinking is, *She is young and good-looking, and, besides, she is the cause of all the difficulties with my family. She will certainly make out all right if she ever gets bored with me.*

The second greatest problem the young rival encounters, and one which comes as the greatest surprise to the woman he left behind, is the lack of love and affection. In general, young people are more affectionate than older ones, and often women need more tenderness than men. The young woman with her older lover who, don't forget, also suffers from guilt feelings over leaving his wife and children is really not to be envied.

The wear and tear sets in more rapidly in the extramarital relationship than in a marriage. The husband constantly draws comparisons between his wife and his girlfriend, and consciously or unconsciously looks for good reasons to leave the younger woman. He holds every little thing against her. He punishes her for every little mistake by getting extremely irritated. Scarcely has she made even the slightest misstep and he thinks: *My God, I made the wrong choice.*

Comparing the five years I spent with this man to the rest of my life, my heart turns cold. It seems unbelievable to me now that I was able to survive with so little affection. There were days when he hardly said a word to me. Whenever we went out, he acted like a stranger. Since we moved in the same circles and went to the same restaurants as friends of his wife, I could understand that he was afraid, but my emotions weren't convinced.

He never held my hand. He never helped me on with my coat, and it was out of the question for him ever to kiss me in public. After dinner in a restaurant he would usually get up from the table and make for the door as if he had completely forgotten about me. If I complained, heartbroken, I got as my answer, "You'll just have to get used to it." If I wasn't satisfied with that, he'd say, "If you don't stop, you'll force me to leave." I was on the way to a mental breakdown.

I barely coped with this during the first year we lived together. Later, I started crying whenever I saw a man helping a woman on with her coat or holding the door for her. I was so starved for affection that it took on really frightening forms.

One spring day during our last year together, I was on my way to the library and felt weak and dispirited, as I had waited up for him until three in the morning. When he finally came home, he told me he had been out for dinner with his Russian business partners. I decided to have something to drink in a small café under the arcade at the end of the Palais Royal gardens. There was a large aviary, and inside it were all kinds of colorful birds. Among them were two so-called inseparables, absolutely charming little things. I couldn't take my eyes off them, they were so affectionate with one another.

I don't remember how long I sat there and stared at them. But I do remember that I suddenly burst into tears and couldn't stop sobbing. The waitress sat down next to me and tried to comfort me, but it was half an hour before I was able to lift up my head again. I did lousy work that day.

Sometimes, when I was at my wits' end, I went to the movies. I saw *Harold and Maude* a total of eight times, not only because it is a story of true love and, in my opinion, one of the most beautiful films of our time, but because of one scene in particular that renewed my strength for hours afterward. It is evening. Harold and Maude are sitting next to one another along the seashore. You see only their silhouettes against the evening sky, and Harold slowly lays his head on Maude's shoulder. That is all.

Today, I don't understand why this film filled me with so many emotions. (It is among the modern classics and for years has been playing in one or another of the small cinemas in the Latin Quarter.) At that time these emotions were lifesaving to me.

If there was any comfort in this hopeless situation, and comfort is a bad word, it was only that all the men in our circle behaved in a similar fashion. All of us young women had the same problems. We felt like hangers-on, completely unimportant. A solidarity of sorts evolved among us: One would try to cheer the other one. We all cursed the wives who made our lives so difficult, and we didn't understand that it was the men who were at fault. If these greedy women would finally make reasonable demands, then a divorce could be only a few months away. What we didn't understand was that the decision to divorce depended entirely on the men, and they simply didn't want to make it.

As I've said before, the young rival's greatest handicap is her youth. It is her inexperience that allows her to cling to an illusion, to promises, to single sentences thrown at her that are not meant to be serious and have only one aim: to smoothe things over. The young mistress has no legal rights. She is, in the most literal sense of the word, a decoration, something that a man can show off, stick in his lapel, and then forget.

Of course, part of the problem is that the young woman has to fit into the man's life completely. What she wants doesn't count. Her concepts about the future, her efforts in her profession or her academic work are secondary. She is told time and again that the man is the center of the universe. "Just be happy that you've got a successful guy like me to take care of you." he tells her. If she expects any consideration, especially of her feelings, she's whistling in the dark.

An example: On most evenings we spent with our circle of friends, the women sat around silently and listened to the men talk. What about? About their families. It didn't occur to them that this topic was terribly painful for us. They wanted only one thing: to show one another just what good and thoughtful providers they were. Then they preened themselves on their latest conquests: us.

"Look at me," Simon used to brag. He was a high-ranking bureaucrat in an international organization. "My whole salary goes to my wife and children. Here I sit and let my friend, who is only half my age, support me." Georgina had just turned twenty-five and worked as an assistant for a wire service. She had been Simon's secretary and had earned a good salary. As their affair became common knowledge, she had had to quit her job. She now earned only half her previous salary. When Simon had left his wife, his friends had lent him the money to pay for an apartment. But Georgina had been footing the household expenses for seven years.

On these social evenings, which were absolute torture for us, there was a lot of drinking, and this usually lasted until the early morning hours. We sat there like good little girls, silently watching, as we had run out of things to say long ago. Every one of us had but one thought: *How do I get my man to leave?* Pleas went unheeded; nor would it help if we got up and left. Very often we fell asleep in armchairs in various bars or apartments. And when we woke up at six o'clock in the morning, nobody had missed us at all. The slurred voices were just as loud. The air was so heavy with smoke you could hardly breathe, and the talk was still the same: the dissatisfied wife, how expensive it was to send the children to private schools, and how many girlfriends had preceded us.

The wife knows something the young mistress refuses to acknowledge: that she isn't the only woman he's interested in. If a man leaves his wife for a girlfriend, it doesn't mean that he plans to be faithful to her. Why should he? A man who needs two women is used to lying. One woman more or less makes no difference.

The men in our circle didn't even try to cover up their further indiscretions. They discussed them quite openly when their girlfriends weren't around. Simon told me once, in minute detail, just how he planned to seduce his boss's secretary. He had laid out a battle plan much like a schoolboy's and was terribly proud of his strategy. He was certain of its success.

"What about Georgina?" I asked naïvely. "Don't you love her any more?"

"That has nothing to do with it," he said, looking pityingly at me. "That's only for amusement. Georgina is for keeps."

Life is complicated and full of extremes. If it didn't hurt so much, you could laugh about it. Picture the wife sitting at home, complaining of being bored. The girlfriend, on the other hand, has to go out, like it or not. Going out and watching the man drink himself silly is part of her duties. No matter how much Georgina would plead, when Simon was sitting tight in a restaurant, he was there for the duration. She never dared leave him alone and go home. First of all, she wouldn't be able to sleep. Secondly, she knew what the consequences would be: He'd go on a drinking binge through the shady bars of the Place Pigalle. Once she had left early—she didn't see Simon for two days. Nobody knew where he was. When he was finally found, he was unconscious in the street in front of a whorehouse. He had to be taken to a hospital to be treated for a severe case of alcohol poisoning. It took a year for Georgina to work out a method for getting Simon home before it was too late. She showed me one night. We had had supper in a restaurant, and the men were displaying unmistakable signs of restlessness: one small cognac with coffee, then a double to wash it down, then a beer, then some more wine, and so it went.

Georgina and I exchanged knowing glances. She was pale with fatigue. She simply had to get home. She had a hard day behind her and had to get up early in order to interview workers striking in the suburbs. As her pleading fell on deaf ears, she went to the ladies room and didn't come back. After ten minutes I went to look for her. She was leaning against the mirrored wall of the washroom with her eyes closed. When she saw me, she slipped to the floor without a word and lay there, motionless.

I knew it was all play-acting, but I went along with it. Simon appeared to sense this, too, for he wasn't at all excited when I went to get him. In spite of this, however, he changed his mind, called a taxi, and took Georgina home. The next day I ran into him on the street, and he told me something that made me feel Georgina's time was running out.

"If I only knew what to do with Joan [his wife]," he said, "then I would marry Georgina."

"Because you can't live without her?" I asked.

"No," he explained to me, "because then she'd have the security of marriage and wouldn't get so upset each time I plan to have a little affair."

In short, Simon and Georgina didn't marry; they split. Georgina went back to London, and Simon was taken back by his wife. He promised to reform. He sold the apartment in which he and Georgina had lived. What did Georgina get out of this, she who wanted nothing more fervently than to get married and have four children? Seven years invested in the wrong man.

The logical questions of course are, "Why didn't she see through him earlier? Why does a young woman put up with such treatment? Why didn't she give him a kick in the behind?" The answer is simple: because she had lost her self-confidence. The young mistress had heard for too long, from a man she initially trusted, that she was a nobody; that she had nothing, was nothing, and never would make anything of herself; that she could thank her lucky stars that she was protected; that there was no better life for her.

These tactics work most of the time. In fact, they are the same that have kept generations of wives in line. Add a few promises of divorce and remarriage and you'll have your girlfriend at your mercy for at least five years! (Then she'll get smart.)

Georgina simply shared the fate of many young women who have loved and trusted married men. Simon never even dreamed of leaving his wife. She was part of the Paris literary scene, had written a book on the French Revolution, and was an excellent pianist. Simon wanted to keep sharing her prestige. Even when he was with Georgina's circle of young friends, bragging to anyone who cared to listen about how he had made a slave out of a twenty-five-year-old woman, he was still at heart deeply bound to his wife. She would wait it out, and he knew it. She was a Roman Catholic and belonged to the generation that didn't believe in divorce. In addition, they had four children.

In general, the younger the rival, the greater the chance that the affair will not end in marriage. The man is too afraid. He is scared he'll be left alone when he is old, he refuses to risk his security, not to mention the material goods that he has acquired in the course of his marriage.

If the girlfriend is very much younger, the intellectual difference, her lack of experience, and her lower level of education might be enough to tire the man. Her conversation bores him; he'll talk to her less and less. The old saw that men love dumb women is wrong. Men are generally smarter than we give them credit for being. Only dumb men want dumb women. A demanding man wants and needs a mentally stimulating partner. In the long run, a man will be paralyzed by a woman with whom he can't talk, no matter how admiringly she looks up to him.

During my first two years in Paris, I lived near the Opéra. The apartment next door belonged to a bank director. It was really his second residence, since he and his family lived in a big house in the country. They used the apartment when they went to the opera and didn't want to drive back home that night, or when relatives came to Paris to go shopping, or when they had the strange desire to spend a weekend in the city.

You might, of course, assume that the apartment served other purposes—as a setting for undisturbed trysts, for example—but this wasn't the case. In the entire two years I lived in the building, I never once saw Monsieur Renaux enter his apartment with a woman other than his wife.

When you knew Madame Renaux, you understood. I became friends with her right from the start. She was a heavy woman—not by American but by French standards—in her late fifties, with a very full mouth and laughing eyes. She was generous, lent me table lamps and dishes whenever I had unexpected guests, and in between gave me tips on how to be happily married.

No one would have doubted her expertise in this field. You could see that she was happy. She made no secret of her love for her husband and two grown sons. "I'm not afraid of growing old either," she confided to me, "because I know what it's all about: *esprit,* or spirit. I keep my men amused. They've never been bored with me for a second. I collect interesting stories, and, thank heavens, I've been blessed with a good sense of humor. When we dine together, we sometimes talk and laugh for hours. We openly discuss all our problems. And when my husband comes back from a business trip, do you know what he says? 'I was so bored again without you,' and I believe him."

In order to have a really good partnership, one of the cardinal rules is to be able to talk and laugh together. But what if you have totally different backgrounds? No comparable education, no common interests, no complementary senses of humor? You can, obviously, have a good time for one night, even when there's an intellectual gap, but sooner or later the fabric of the relationship will wear thin. Solid marriages are built on long-lasting intellectual stimulation and real understanding.

The communication problem is often very hard to overcome, even between people of the same age. Between an older man and a much younger woman, however, the inability to communicate often means the beginning of the end. And it is more painful, usually, than for an older woman and her younger lover. The reason is that men are more impatient than women and miss no opportunity to flaunt their "superiority." This is catastrophic for a young mistress. How often does she have to hear, "Oh, you don't know." How many sentences begin with, "Of course, you wouldn't understand, but this is the way things are. . . ." I don't need to mention just how devastating this is for a young person's self-esteem. What is the result when the young girlfriend is too discouraged to defend herself? She becomes even more subservient, more his doormat, and is taken less and less seriously. The relationship loses its intensity, and the man's complete loss of interest is imminent.

Now to the subject of "looking for one's lost youth." Women who have younger boyfriends usually behave in a very discreet fashion. Not so men, who go about trying to recapture their youth with a vengeance. The consequences, of course, are that the age difference becomes even more brutally apparent.

My friend in Paris insisted on going to the worst kind of discothèques where there were only very young people "so you can't say you don't get around anymore because of me." To be perfectly honest, I never would have gone to those seedy clubs anyway, and the effect of seeing a well-dressed, gray-haired man among a clientele consisting mainly of schoolboys, junkies, and an occasional student was just as embarrassing as you can imagine. What was worse, he insisted on being as conspicuous as possible, dragging me out onto the empty dance floor and calling everybody's attention to us. To top it off, he was a pretty rotten dancer, and if he saw anybody laughing at us, he was so insulted he'd want to pick a fight right then and there. I could have died on the spot.

Of course, he hadn't the slightest idea of the ritual that prevailed in such places. He didn't know about the unwritten rule of letting those generally acknowledged as the best dancers take the floor first, the others dancing only when the commotion was such that nobody would notice them. But, had he known, he wouldn't have cared. He *wanted* to be the center of attention and was surprised when all he got was laughter and hostility. Sometimes he tried to force a good mood by drinking too much and buying a round for the entire group at our table. But it never worked. The crowd remained hostile. Most of these evenings ended with the pronouncement, "Well, I was the oldest person there again," followed by days of bad temper. Despite this, he wouldn't stop going to those hangouts.

A much greater problem, however, is jealousy. If nothing else destroys the relationship between a married man and his young mistress, jealousy will do the trick. The girlfriend is torn apart by jealousy of the wife, and the husband is madly jealous of his girlfriend—for two reasons: first, because of his insecurity (a younger man might please her more); and, secondly, because he himself is constantly unfaithful. He betrays his wife with his young friend, and the young friend with his wife. And he believes others do as he does. It's a vicious circle, and a classic example of self-deception.

In most relationships between older married men and young women, the mistrust is so tangible you can almost *see* it floating in midair. It poisons everything. Simon was completely convinced that, when Georgina flew off to London to be with her parents (which didn't happen very often because there wasn't enough money), she was visiting a former boyfriend. Why? Because, scarcely had she turned her back, Simon was off to see his wife and stay there overnight.

When Georgina's father became ill and she had to fly home, the absurdity of Simon's jealousy came to a head. Shortly before, somebody had given Georgina a dog, which became a thorn in Simon's side, as he was envious of every friendly glance his mistress bestowed on the little pet. When Georgina left, Simon refused to feed the animal. He called her up and said: "The dog is starving!" The poor animal would surely not have survived if Simon's son, who happened by the apartment to get some records, hadn't felt sorry for him and taken him home.

Simon didn't spend a single day in the apartment while Georgina was gone. He explained that he was afraid; he said he didn't want to be in a place where nobody was there to take care of him while his girlfriend was having a good time in London.

Jealousy is more or less a problem for us all. Baseless jealousy, however, is very hurtful and becomes unbearable after a while. I well remember the first vacation I spent with my friend. It was on an island in the Mediterranean. We stayed with an Italian family and had to collect our mail from a nearby harbor town. He did this because, he claimed, he could maneuver the car better over the hilly roads. His real reason, however, was that he wanted to make sure I didn't see the letters he received from his wife. He lied to me, telling me there was no longer any contact between them, and I, out of inexperience, believed him.

To him, letters meant lies, and when one day I got a letter from my brother, he created a big scene. He handed me the envelope with a threatening look, and as I started to open it he began to yell. My eagerness to open the letter simply proved that I didn't care for his company. Couldn't I at least wait until after lunch? Was the letter really from my brother? He doubted it. I cheated on him, I was ungrateful and untrustworthy. Late that evening, as I finally got up enough courage to read the letter, I learned that my mother was ill and in the hospital.

I spent a sleepless night and vowed to call home the next morning. I did so, but, as a consequence, my friend didn't speak a word to me for three days. He was convinced that everything was a lie, that the letter was from another man, that we were hatching a plot against him, that I was only looking for an excuse to get away from him in order to go back to some boyfriend in Vienna. It took days to calm him down.

The "ex-friend" is a subject all its own. Although he usually doesn't even exist, he is very detrimental to the relationship. Older married men usually can't believe that their young girlfriends haven't any past worth talking about. They themselves consist of nothing else. Their wives are always on their minds, and since they judge others by their own conduct, they are convinced the younger woman has a former lover who continues to be in the picture.

I suffered terribly under the pressure of such suspicions, and they slowly killed off my love for my friend. He, of course, thought he had good reasons for his doubts. One Sunday when he was home with me (his family had gone on a ski trip), an architect from Vienna whom I barely knew called me up. He had gotten my number from a mutual friend and asked me where he could stay the four days he was to be in Paris.

I had barely uttered two sentences when I noticed that my friend was standing behind me, getting more furious by the minute. Whenever I spoke German he always suspected the worst. In order to calm him down I told him exactly who it was and what he wanted. "Do you think I'm a complete idiot?" he thundered. "That's your former lover. He knows that you're usually alone on Sundays and wants to meet you." He fell into a raging fury that lasted for an entire half hour until he was actually foaming at the mouth. He brought up the "ex-friend" from that day on every time we had an argument. One evening, when I came home from the library a bit later than usual, he said without hesitation, "Aha, you've been out with your old boyfriend again."

Jealousy is the greatest ally a wife can have. She has

191

no idea of the tortures suffered by her unfaithful husband and cannot imagine her younger rival's anguish when she discovers that her lover has been visiting his family behind her back. There are always informants, whether they be well-meaning friends or the husband's secretary, who want to tell the young woman about the latest "outrage" while it's still hot off the presses: He bought new clothes for his wife and children; his new suit cost a fortune; he has planned an expensive summer vacation for his family in Greece; on those afternoons he's supposed to have been in the office, he has been playing tennis with his wife; he took his wife to an office dinner and she went with him on a business trip to Brussels. . . .

It's terrible when the mistress finds out things aren't the way she was told. That actually, there never was a clean break between them. He says to his wife, "Don't worry, I'm always available during the day, and otherwise everything will stay the same—the only difference is that I won't come home every night." The version he tells his mistress is: "Everything is finished. I'm only in contact with the children. I communicate with my wife only through our lawyers."

Even when mutual friends don't say anything, it finally dawns on the young woman that she's being had. For the first time, she thinks about leaving. Those lonely weekends become even more painful, and the so-called family days are in the end unbearable. Even when the relationship has settled into a certain routine, the allegedly powerful rival is never sure whether her friend will come back to her after a family Sunday. If he doesn't return until after midnight, she's definitely been counting the hours since supper, painting fearful pictures in her mind. She has no idea what really is happening, and always fears the worst.

If it weren't so tragic, the whole thing would be laughable. It is incomprehensible why men choose to heap such burdens on themselves. The much-feared family Sunday usually follows this script: The husband appears at the family home; his reception is icy. In order to relieve the tense atmosphere, he and the children flee to the safety of the movies, the swimming pool, or to play soccer; and slowly the ice thaws.

Once he has the children on his side, he can venture safely back to the house where, after a period of time, his wife will agree to indulge in conversation. By suppertime the old family feeling is back, and it remains so until the children's bedtime.

Finally, when the two of them are alone, they start with a neutral theme, such as money or problems with the children—how much the new school satchel cost or what the dentist said. In order to relax, they have a couple of drinks, and then they get to the real heart of the matter. The husband speaks of his hopes for the future and, in order to emphasize their togetherness, brings forth old memories. He talks about his in-laws. Then the conversation becomes more animated. The husband feels he really belongs here, but, in spite of everything, after a couple of hours he gets up and prepares to leave. Then the wife asks the dreaded question: "It was almost like old times again. Why do you have to go?" The parting is then as frosty as the greeting. The circle closes, and the following Sunday it starts all over again. When the husband gets home to his mistress, he usually finds her in tears and has to comfort her. Not an easy life at all.

It is at this point that most relationships between an older married man and his young girlfriend break up. Usually it's the young mistress who calls it quits. But it is tough. She can't count on anyone to help her. Young men

193

of her own age now appear uneducated and immature. The only person who could help is the wife. If the wife were to begin to fight at this point and say, "I won't wait a day longer; you have to choose between her or me," she'd win in a walk. But most of them don't fight because they don't know what's going on in the other relationship, because they overestimate the strength of the affair and are too afraid of losing their husbands altogether. What does happen? The wife remains passive, the husband is not about to let either woman slip from his grasp if he can help it, and the affair continues, sometimes for years, until the younger woman finally gets up her courage and leaves. But until she reaches that point, she has wasted an enormous amount of time and energy, and all those involved have been terribly hurt.

The greatest mistake a deserted wife can make is to be overcome by self-pity. The second biggest mistake is to feel too proud to get to know the mistress: "I don't want to have anything to do with that person" is a silly notion. The wife could outdo the younger rival, but only by getting to know her and by finding out through her how stable the "illicit" relationship really is. It would be wrong to blame an inexperienced young woman for the entire unhappy business. The cliché of the clever rival who entices the poor husband away from his happy home doesn't hold water. If the wife wants to win, she has to analyze the situation and learn to say, "This was my husband's fault, that hers, and this mine."

The wife knows her husband. Now it's a question of getting to know the girlfriend. She must find out which of the two is the least able to bear up under the pressure, which one will give in first. If the mistress shows signs of exhaustion, then the wife concentrates on her. If it's the

194

husband, she should try to force him to come to a decision.

Men are not that strong. The wife will soon realize that her husband is also suffering, that he is much weaker than she assumed, and that he is plagued by his conscience. He probably can't sleep for nights on end, takes tranquilizers for weeks at a time, and wants nothing more badly than to have things as they once were.

The wife is also usually completely unaware of just how much influence she exerts on the new relationship. She plays an important and constant role, even though she may do nothing directly, and that presence can become unbearable to the young mistress. Her husband will definitely talk about her at great length.

Men tend to torture women with their previous marriages or love affairs. Young men gossip much more about amorous adventures than do girls. They rave in great detail about their conquests, boast about their former girlfriends' gorgeous legs and wild orgasms. The current girlfriends often get the feeling that the only time they'll really be appreciated will be after the affair has ended. Many men simply are not able to enjoy what they have, adoring only those women they can't possess. The wife's greatest plus is that she has been taken out of the running, so to speak, and therefore, as bizarre as it may seem, she becomes more desirable than ever before. Another plus for the wife: She has patience, and time. The mistress, on the other hand, gets more and more nervous with every year she remains unmarried. Add to this the well-meant advice from her friends and relatives who warn, "You're wasting your life; he'll never get a divorce," (and you know that she won't wait forever).

Many men need an astonishingly long time before

they're ready to become part of another person's feelings. Even after living together for a year or two, the two are often still strangers. However long he's been with the girl-friend, he's known his wife at least ten years longer. He also knows that his wife long ago ceased to function as an individual; she thinks of herself as part of the clan. She's the mother of his children and has learned to consider his money as family money. To him, this spells security. His young friend, however, has spent most of her life without him. In comparison to his wife, she is a stranger whom he still mistrusts.

The wife also holds the stronger moral position. For hundreds of years men have pigeonholed women as either good or bad, virtuous or sensual, reliable or exciting, dis-ciplined or passionate, and so on. As fascinated as some men can be by their new friends, they would never list them under the heading "good." The husband has no great opinion of what he's doing. He knows he is playing a bru-tal game and is contemptuous of himself—even if he doesn't plan to change his ways. A woman who is ready to go along with the game is guilty by association, literally, and thus just as much an object of his scorn.

The longer the triangular relationship endures, the more the wife in question becomes the Madonna, while her young rival becomes sexual temptation personified. Who wants to marry a woman of easy virtue? The girlfriend naturally feels this, and the more she pushes, trying to take over the wife's place, the clearer this becomes. The image of the good versus the evil woman is so strong in some men that it distorts reality. The mistress can by na-ture be a model of kindness and sincerity, but it won't help her very much. The fact remains that she was "the cause" of the husband's leaving his family so she is basi-cally "no good." Naturally, the husband has little interest in giving her a chance: He already has one Madonna and doesn't need two. When a man tells his girlfriend: "How can you compare yourself to my wife?" She should know that there is no hope.

And then there are the man's guilt feelings. Many men seem to have cornered the market on guilt. They indulge in it with a strange, almost perverse joy. They suffer so much guilt that the atmosphere in the second household reeks of it. Yet, they don't change their ways. Guilt feelings are often used as an excuse, of course. When the husband gets drunk, for instance, he complains: "I had to do this. Otherwise I wouldn't be able to stand it." When he spends time or money on the family but ignores his mistress, he says, "I withdrew my love, but nobody will be able to say I let them starve as well."

Because he feels guilty, the husband often tries to shift as much blame as he possibly can onto his girlfriend. Sometimes he even succeeds in putting the whole burden entirely on her shoulders. The younger she is and the less experienced, the more she lets herself be convinced that she alone is responsible for the mess they're all in; that she has failed; that, instead of bringing this man a new and happy life, she has brought him misfortune. If she is a strong person, she simply tallies up the balance sheet and leaves. If she is weak, the necessary impulse for ending the affair could come from the wife if she has been correctly informed as to the status of the relationship. Most wives, however, are much too passive. They wait for their husbands to make up their own minds—and perhaps one in a hundred actually does that. What they don't know is that, after the first blush of happiness with the young rival, a man caught between two women will generally welcome a decision that brings him domestic peace.

Another area that causes the wife much suffering and

gives her so many dreadful moments is sex. The torture that so many wives put themselves through is really absurd. One thing has to be made clear: If there's a good physical relationship between husband and wife, the marriage will survive just about any crisis. There may be affairs but never a serious threat. If the couple is compatible sexually, and the marriage is suffering only from signs of wear and tear, there is always hope. Their physical separation in terms of living arrangements lets the husband see his wife in a different light, since the day-to-day fights are waged with another.

The fact that he has to fight for every chance to see his wife—and each time he does so he may also have to contend with his mistress's bad mood or tearful outbreaks—only makes the wife more desirable. He remembers his fascination with her at the start of their relationship; he makes more and more comparisons; and, finally, the fear of losing his wife becomes unbearable. The result: The sooner his wife threatens a complete break, the quicker the erring husband returns home.

The only marriages that are seriously threatened by a lover are those that were bad to begin with—marriages undertaken because the young people wanted to get away from their parents, marriages where either partner thought he or she was getting a "good catch," or those hurried into it because a child was on its way. Threatened are relationships in which there is neither intellectual nor physical compatibility, unions in which two people live side by side but not together. These marriages hardly deserve to remain intact. Very often the husbands haven't come near their wives in years. They have led married lives in which sex was a swear word and eroticism nonexistent. Despite this, a man may want to stay in such a marriage to keep his comforts, peace and quiet. The wife might stay to ensure financial security in her old age, not to mention her material comforts in the present; there's hardly a man alive who will willingly divide house and property and make do with half. That's why the mistress will have to go if the wife threatens divorce.

Nothing lasts forever. Even when the physical attraction between husband and girlfriend is extraordinarily strong, when at the start they nearly live in bed, who is to say it's going to be like this for all eternity?

For two people to find that their bodies are perfectly matched, that they "click" as we say, is a small miracle in itself. But after the first euphoria dies down, they have to work just as hard as any other couple on their relationship.

The body plays a very important part in life, but the mind plays an even more significant one. If there is nothing more between two people than a good, healthy physical attraction, the future is in jeopardy. A man rarely imagines that a woman's physical desire for him can wane faster than his for her. And yet it is true. If he is mentally cruel, his sex appeal will vanish. Mind and body are intimately connected. You can't hurt the one and expect the other to love you for it. If a man wounds a woman too often, she'll soon lose all desire to sleep with him.

Men and women don't seem to have the same reactions, especially where arguments and fights are concerned. For many men, quarrels are nothing more than a welcome bit of stimulation. You scream, you threaten, you hate one another for the sole purpose of making up again and enjoying lovemaking twice as much. Not so for a woman, at least not in the long run. She might feel some erotic stimulation at the beginning of the affair because she's afraid she'll lose the man, but if fighting, yelling, and irritation become part of everyday life, she won't want to sleep with him for long.

Women are much more sensitive to words than are men. When they say something, they usually mean it. They often wait a long time before speaking their minds, but once that mind is made up, they go straight ahead and do whatever they said they would. Men, on the other hand, love to play poker. They don't expect the woman to take seriously every word, every accusation they throw at her during a fight. They like to provoke, to bluff. They throw in the ace and wait to see what happens. They don't realize that they have convinced the woman everything is finished. They are surprised by her "exaggerated" reaction. "Don't make such a fuss," they declare. "Come on, I'll show you a good time in bed." That she needs love and not a "good time" escapes them.

For a young woman and an older married man, fights can turn very vicious. The man very often quarrels just as much with his young friend as he has done with his wife. Sometimes even more. And every fight propels them farther apart. When he threatens to go back to his wife, the girlfriend believes him. She does not know that he isn't serious and only wants to provoke a reaction. In the long run, this can't be good. The husband is bluffing, while the mistress takes every word seriously and becomes more and more hurt and withdrawn. In the end money problems, lies, guilt feelings, jealousies, fights, and arguments grind on the erotic desires of the young woman, while such conflict seems to have far less effect on the man.

So what happens? The husband simply doesn't realize, or refuses to recognize, what's going on. He keeps insisting on sleeping with her. If he notices her resistance, he gets angry. Is this why he left his wife, to be frustrated by his mistress? Is it all worth the trouble? As a result, the young rival complies, fakes desire and orgasm, and slowly but surely begins to lose respect for herself and for him.

For a time this may suffice. But, finally, any man who has even a touch of sensitivity will realize what's going on. More fights follow, more more distrust and jealousy (does she have another lover?), and the beginning of the end is at hand.

If the wife would only screw up her courage and talk to her husband's mistress as early as possible—not in hysterics and tears or with threats, but quite simply as person to person—many a rival would break off the relationship, perhaps not right away but at least earlier than she would have done otherwise. Remember, the younger woman hears arguments only from one side, the husband's. These arguments usually convince her that the wife is a monster. And to hurt a monster is all right!

There is a certain rule that applies to most relationships between husband and mistress. Their happiest time is at the beginning, when the wife knows nothing. The husband usually has built up some credit by being a "good boy" for a while, and he can stay out late without arousing suspicion. To his mistress, this "freedom" proves that the marriage is on the rocks (as indeed he has told her).

At the beginning then, he shows up four or five times a week and is able to remain constantly in touch with her. The young rival remains optimistic even at the second stage of the relationship—that is, when the wife has discovered the affair and is still too shaken to react. As long as the wife maintains that I-don't-want-to-know-a-thing attitude and hopes against hope that the affair will dissolve like a bad dream of it own accord, everything is great for the husband and the younger woman. It is only when the wife starts to fight back that the shadows begin to fall.

201

But, unfortunately, most wives fight with too little energy and conviction and jump into battle much too late.

The most successful way to get rid of the younger rival is to throw your husband out of the house. It works out best for everybody concerned. It should really happen at the beginning of the affair, as soon as the wife has found out what is going on and, if possible, before the husband and his girlfriend have grown used to one another.

The most drastic method is the most effective: Pack his things in his suitcase, put it in front of the door or in his office, and then change the lock. You don't listen to any arguments, you decline every opportunity to talk, and even forbid him to contact the children. The shock will bring him around.

My friend Greta from New York put this theory into practice with great success, but it took a lot of courage because she still loved her husband. Despite this, she felt she had no other choice. For four years he had carried on an affair with his secretary, and she never knew a thing. He came home late every now and then, but never stayed out the whole night. Suddenly he didn't come home for two and three nights in a row, and she discovered to her complete horror that he had taken an apartment with the other woman.

When Greta confronted him with her knowledge, he admitted the affair but tried to smooth it over with, "Don't worry. I'll spend more time with you than with her, and the weekends will be all for you and the children."

Greta waited for exactly ten days. She needed that amount of time to sort things out. She had been married for twelve years, was extremely attractive, and had a figure a bathing beauty could be proud of. She had never been unfaithful to her husband. They had always had a good sex life and had slept together up until the time of the revelation. She had, however, suffered three miscarriages in the seven years that elapsed between the birth of her daughter and that of her son, and during those seven years she had been less interested in sex. That was when the affair started.

The secretary was pale and thin and no match for Greta who was a successful interior decorator. Greta thought the following: *If he is going to leave me for that woman after twelve years, then the sooner the better.* After a dreadful scene, she threw her husband and all of his clothes out of the house. The result: Over the following six weeks it became clear to him that, although he had not been able to admit it to himself before, Greta was the only woman for him, and he couldn't live without her and the children.

Take this as a rule of thumb: If a man is forced into a choice between two women, and if his marriage hasn't completely eroded, he'll always choose his wife, as she is generally the one in whom he has the most trust.

If a wife is too weak to fight, she'll have to sit it out, and the effects will be much more painful. She'll have to wait until her husband has worn himself out, until all of the previously described money, communication, love, and jealousy problems have taken their toll and destroyed his relationship with his lover, and this can take years.

But here, too, to bring the actual end about, the wife has to make all the decisions and act as the driving force. She can do this by trying to set up a meeting with the younger woman, but to succeed she must remain calm and completely honest. If she's afraid, she must just remember that the young rival is even more afraid. Remember that even if the rival appears strong and experienced, she must be unhappy and weak because she is in a hopeless situation. If there's a chance that the husband will eventually return home, the wife should waste no time telling the mistress. Nothing wears out a young woman's patience faster than a wife who is sure of herself and tells her in a sincere and civil fashion that the marriage is still alive, that they still sleep together, and that she knows he'll come back to her.

In my case a meeting between the wife of my American friend and me took place. The only problem was that it came at a hopeless moment. It was much too late. I had already been living with the man for two years, and we had grown accustomed to each other even though we were far from being blissfully happy. All three of us had become so demoralized by this time, we simply couldn't come to any decision.

I met his wife at noontime in a small café near the library where I studied. I was so nervous that, as I saw her, I knocked a bread basket off the table with my elbow. After the initial formalities, I noticed to my relief that she was just as overwrought as I was. She was so shaky she could hardly speak. We tried to be friendly and plunged right away into a debate over literature. Neither of us dared to mention our man's name. Our meeting lasted for perhaps three quarters of an hour. Finally, she accompanied me back to the library, where I explained to her how to use the card catalogue. During the entire time, not a word passed our lips about our common problem. Neither of us had any strength left. We had suffered too much and our fears were too great. When my lover found out about this meeting, he was furious. Of course, he was afraid we had teamed up against him. And that's what we should have done. During the last three years he and I spent together, there was no further talk of divorce. Every time the subject came up, he reacted with a deep sigh. What would become of the children? He was the one who had brought them to Europe, and he would have to bring them back to the States again. When I finally left him, his wife could have won him back, but she no longer cared to. She filed for divorce a year later.

In order to have a good marriage, one that is safe from younger—and older—rivals (and, of the two, the older is much more dangerous), you always have to fight. A lot of life is spent fighting, whether we like it or not. This is the world in which we live and to which we have to accommodate ourselves. A wife who is confronted by a young rival—and it is a comfort to know that it doesn't really happen that often—has to overcome her hurt and her pride, and fight. She now knows where the soft spots lie and has a good chance of winning.

What else is there to do? Just one more thing: Dump an old cliché on the garbage pile—that of the happy, victorious, self-assured, spoiled, and coddled "other woman" who is favored over the wife simply because she is younger. This creature does not exist, except perhaps in the world of romantic fiction of no literary merit.

In reality the mistress is a person who is more to be pitied than envied, who wants desperately to get out of the trap she is in, who'll never ever consent to be the "other woman" again. Why? Because it was the most painful experience of her whole life.

8

Discerning Fiction from Fact and Learning a New Vocabulary

In the summer of 1978, President Jimmy Carter passed a new law that, as of January 1, 1979, no man or woman in the United States under the age of seventy could be forced to retire. This is probably just the first step for new legislation that will make it illegal for employers to retire anyone solely because of age. Representative Claude Pepper, a Florida Democrat, chairman of the Select Committee on Aging, and the driving force behind this new law, will be eighty-two this year and is still going strong. Singer Pearl Bailey, who is in her mid-sixties, supported Pepper at a three-hour hearing in Washington last September, emphasizing the point that age discrimination is absurd in a country that has elected a seventy-year-old man as its president.

The pattern seems obvious to me. Whether we realize it or not, we are turning our backs on the youth cult. We have stopped lumping people together in age groups and are beginning to realize that everyone of us is an individual with his or her own biological truth. People simply age differently, as you can see for yourself by merely looking around. Some people are already old at sixty, others still attractive and productive at the age of eighty. The American vocabulary already reflects this fact, and we speak of a "young forty," a "very young fifty"—but also of an "old thirty-five" when a person of that age has lost all youthfulness and the spirit has aged before its time.

Getting older is like swimming, skiing, and taking exams: You simply can't allow yourself to get nervous about it. If you're afraid, you're at a disadvantage and you start out behind the eight ball. If you're not afraid, you can only win. You're as young as you feel. If some envious person tries to put you down, ignore that person. Each one of us has only one criterion by which to judge—our own private and personal standards. We must live by our own convictions since we have, first and foremost, to live with ourselves. If you think of yourself as beautiful, if you like to see your face, put up mirrors throughout your living quarters just to please yourself. Should well-meaning acquaintances question your actions by saying, "You really are vain, and at your age," your answer should be a cool: "Which age do you mean? I know that I'm finally old enough to do what I want."

Never let yourself be intimidated. The times have changed. Do what you think is best for you and forget about: "What would people say?" You have to believe in yourself and in your life. If you let yourself be persuaded you're old, you'll suddenly behave as if you are. You'll radiate "old," and you'll eventually be regarded as old by everybody around you.

You have to learn to value your own worth and to see to it that others do the same. You have to be realistic and understand that much of life is a business venture. You know, of course, that the value of houses and works of art depends on heating up the demand, on hard-nosed negotiations, and on emphasis on quality. But there's one thing

207

many of us don't realize, and that is that we also have to constantly "sell" ourselves. Nobody wants a loser. Everybody much prefers people who are energetic, optimistic, successful, and full of life. You have to stop complaining and learn to think positively, primarily about yourself.

Let me give you an example of how not to go about it: A friend who was separated from her husband moaned about her bad luck with men. She's red-haired, in her late thirties, has a pretty face and a good figure. As she was receiving a relatively generous allowance from her husband, she had enough money to dress well. At first glance she is extraordinarily attractive, and nobody could believe she had not been able to find a lover for the past six months.

After a single evening with her, however, I knew why she was still alone. She "sold" herself so poorly, I wanted to cry. In the fourteen years she was married, her husband had made her so insecure that she simply couldn't imagine anybody could find her desirable. Unfortunately, she managed to convince others of that as well, time and again.

I had invited her and two men I knew to spend an evening at my place. She had a good time, hit it off right away with the architect I had invited for her, and after dinner we were all in such a good mood we decided to go to a discothèque.

On the way there she became visibly upset. She didn't say a word in the car, and once we had parked she suddenly announced, "If you'd like, I'll just stay here in the car." General astonishment. She continued, "Didn't you people see that two young women got out over there and went into the discothèque by themselves? They're obviously looking for company." We looked at her, not understanding at all.

"But we're already spoken for," the architect said.

At that, she got out. But on the way to the door of the club, she hesitated again. "Do you really want to go in there with me? There are only young girls inside. They'll stare when they see who you're with."

That's the way it went all evening, even though the crowd was a good one and was not in fact made up of youngsters; she was one of the most attractive women there. At first we tried to contradict her arguments. After an hour we even persuaded her to dance. But she kept coming back to the same theme even in the midst of the most lively entertainment: She was too old to be doing this.

As a result, her self-depreciation won out over her appearance. The evening ended poorly. The architect, who had been very much interested in her at the start, never called. She had "sold herself" wrong. An art dealer who says to a prospective buyer: "The watercolor you seem to like so much is really not particularly attractive and, in fact, the colors will begin to fade in a few years," can never hope to sell the picture, let alone get a good price for it.

If you're feeling unsure of yourself, it's always better to say too little than too much. This brings us to an extremely important point: the use of speech. Words are living things. Barely do they leave our lips than they begin to assume a life of their own. They build us up; they depress us; they make us afraid or happy. In each case they conjure up images, and these images last longer than we realize.

For example, when I hear the word "geezer," I see a palsied little man, the kind you almost never see in real life anymore. When I hear "old crone" I imagine anything but an attractive creature. We have to learn to be more careful in our choice of words and to avoid those that cause unnecessary fear of growing old. The little word "still" is particularly deadly. As harmless as it seems, it can be devastating. It will diminish the most beautiful description, casting a gray shadow over a woman's clear eyes and faultless complexion. "How is she looking these days?" we ask harmlessly. "Still pretty good," is the answer, and the "still" implies "but not for long."

Why can't we be generous? Why not live without the "still"? If we're paying a compliment, then let's do it from the heart and without any hints that we actually mean the opposite. Basically, everything in life is "still." We don't have to make a major issue out of it. We are still healthy, still productive, my children are still alive, my husband still loves me, the sun still rises, and I still don't have cancer. What kind of talk is this? I know that I'll be getting old someday. Nothing lasts forever. But as long as I'm attractive, I'm attractive without the "still." The same goes for everything else.

While we are learning to avoid the use of the word "still" in describing people, we also have to learn to act normally in the company of younger people. An astonishing number of people feel threatened by an age difference of only five or six years and can't refrain from exaggerating the barrier they feel exists. "When you're as old as I am," they say, or, "It's only when I hear you people talk that I realize how old I am." They're in effect forcing the others to think about something that hadn't even occurred to them up to that point, namely the age difference. You have to stop doing that, even if you were only trying to fish for compliments. As I said, words are living things. When you run yourself down, others always have an uneasy feeling. It's an old rule of thumb: Never call attention to your own failings and *especially* not to imaginary ones. Other people aren't going to take the trouble to check out whether these assertions are true or not. "If she says she's old, she must be right," they say. This certainly is not what you had in mind.

Older women, unfortunately, often tend to denigrate not only themselves but all their contemporaries in one fell swoop. They use words such as "old bag," "old lady," or even "broad." They don't realize how much harm they are doing.

Don't ever say: "There are a lot of old women sitting around." Why not "old ladies" instead, which is also a better description. Even in jest, you shouldn't use such phrases as "old wives' tales." Never use a word that purposely makes someone old, that emphasizes somebody's age or detracts from an old person's esteem. Even if you're still very young yourself, you should be sensitive to this. You'll be older soon enough, and then you'll benefit from it, too.

A prime example of self-denigration is the use of the phrase "in my day" or "in my time." If you use it in conversation, you immediately cut yourself off from the rest of the group. You move yourself into another century, not only another age category. I have never understood the phrase. What does "in my day" mean? Or, "in my time things were different"? My time is *now*. As long as I'm alive *this is my time*. From cradle to grave, every second is *my lifetime*. Only a person who has given up all hope and lost all optimism, who no longer has the desire to change anything for the better in this world has the right to say "in my day," meaning in his other youth.

It is also very important *never to lie about your age*. If people ask you, give a precise answer. If you're with a group of relative strangers and you talk about your youth, tell them without batting an eyelash how old you were then and how old you are now. Do not add: "I don't want to sound ancient" or anything of the sort, just remain your natural self, give them the figure and give it with pride. You have to stop treating your age as an incurable disease. If people are surprised at your age, take it as a compliment. If they say, "What, you're fifty-five already?" smile and answer, "Yes, I'm fifty-five, and I assure you it's a very pleasant age, an age you can all look forward to." If, however, you're with a group of people who are *not* interested, then don't force your age upon them.

One of the most elegant American women living, and certainly one of the most beautiful women in the whole world, Carolina Herrera, fashion designer and mother of four, tells everyone who wants to know that she is a grandmother. She herself turns forty-two this year, and it is one of her basic principles never to hide her age. "I don't know why women would want to lie about their age," she told journalists last year. "I am forty-one and, if I say I am thirty-five, then I don't look as good."

During my first visit to Washington, D.C., I had an interesting experience. I was sitting in the restaurant of the beautiful old wing of the National Gallery drinking a cup of coffee. There was an empty seat at the table, and a very pretty young woman sat down with me. I can still see her. She was very slender, almost skinny, had long black hair, and from her complexion I judged her to be of Mediterranean extraction. She had a narrow, intelligent face. The first thing she said to me was, "I'm forty. How old are you?"

As a European I was shocked by her frankness, although this is really one of the most charming American characteristics. I recovered quickly. We then got into a lively debate about life in general and age in particular. She was a sculptor and, on reaching her thirtieth birthday, had decided she had been upset about her age for the last time. "I was then living with a man twelve years younger," she told me, "and on my thirtieth birthday I realized with a shock that in twenty years I'd be fifty and he'd only be thirty-eight. But in the next moment I thought, *Why should I be afraid of a number?* I'm above all that. I am not a number. What does it mean to be fifty? First of all, I'll be me. I am my own flesh and blood. I'll have the same hair and the same eyes, and my cheekbones will be the same. And I was right. Since that birthday, ten years have passed. I'm halfway to fifty now and nothing has changed. Except that I feel better than ever before."

This, of course, is the right way to deal with age. Always remember that the numerical figure cannot harm you. You are above it. Try and dissociate yourself from your "particular age group." You are yourself. If you look and feel young, you *are* young. Never forget: Flesh and blood are stronger than the abstract numbers on birth certificates.

Now for a couple of rules of conduct in society. The first is: Talk. If you're to combat fears of getting older, whenever the subject of age comes up you have to express your opinion, no holds barred. Summon up all your courage, voice your thoughts and feelings, and stand by them.

Don't let anybody confuse you. If you hear a statement such as, "Our landlord is weird; he lives with a woman old enough to be his mother," you reply, "What's so strange about that? Equal rights for all. There are enough women who live with men old enough to be their fathers." If, instead, you sit back and think, "Oh, poor people, what a dumb remark. I could tell you things but it's too much trouble," you haven't advanced the cause one step. It is your duty to open your mouth and you'll see that, before long, you'll profit by it. Your friends will be your first converts. Later, it will be easy to defend aging even in the presence of strangers.

If you're with a group of people you don't know, and you're scared to speak up, tell yourself that these people who seem to present such a unified front sitting there across from you are neither united nor allied. They're not your enemies. They are nothing more than a bunch of more or less insecure individuals. Those who argue most vehemently against you are generally the most quickly convinced and, often, just as they are leaving to go home, they close ranks with you and agree that older women do have more chances in life than the very young.

Jokes are a chapter in themselves. Even when you're in the company of comparative strangers or are invited some place for the first time, you can't allow yourself to laugh at jokes that make fun of old people. If the story is tactless, don't be afraid to say so. If you are insulted by the joke, say so. The one telling it will be ashamed, even if he or she tries to counter with, "Oh, don't be so thin-skinned. I didn't really mean it." But that person *did* mean it. Bad luck if it just didn't work. (If it happens again, the story may be dropped from the repertory).

Another thing on the list of forbidden items: Never tell people what they're thinking of you. You can save yourself remarks such as, "You probably think I'm old as the hills," even when you only mean it jokingly. And when a younger man courts a mature woman, she should accept his attentions quietly, without any great commotion. She will certainly have enough knowledge of human nature to know whether he's serious or not. To bury all chances, from the beginning, by saying, "He obviously thinks I'm much too old for him," is really stupid. The time when a woman was meant only for a man her own age or older is gone. All the doors are open. Do not limit yourself. Women have to stop creating their own barriers and learn to accept greater freedom.

Now, something very important: If you want to keep your peace of mind, if you want to be happy about your age, stop—immediately—being hurt by what people *say*. Concentrate instead on finding out what they *do*. I'll give you an example. The husband of the red-haired woman, the one who destroyed her self-confidence and offered her expensive clothing as consolation, spoke openly of his admiration for teenagers, causing her to dread getting older. Every second word out of his mouth had to do with "sweet sixteen" or a "blonde seventeen-year-old." The women he chased after, however, and with whom he betrayed her, were his own age. Her anxieties were based on theory, not reality. Unfortunately for her, she never learned to distinguish one from the other.

It is particularly enlightening to see what happens when a group of men decide to go out at night to "check out the talent." It's worth going along to watch. The actual conquest, if it is made at all, bears no resemblance to what one might imagine. I had three whole summers to see this for myself.

I worked for a German-language radio station in Italy. We had a small staff, more men than women, and the stuido was located in northern Italy, where there are more tourists in July and August than there are grains of sand on the beach. Night after night, the same scene played itself out: Our male colleagues threw themselves into the night life in order to find happiness among the crowd of female tourists—but only among the youngest and most beautiful, mind you!

Those of us who stayed behind working imagined them in the arms of the most gorgeous creatures or in discothèques full of tanned beauties who swarmed around our radio stars, while the champagne never ceased flowing.

We learned the truth one night when we decided, with a rare convergence of spare time and courage, to catch our heroes in the act. We knew where they were going and surprised them at their last stop, a former ironmongery converted into a dance hall.

What did we find? Not a beauty in sight. Three of our announcers sat at a table by themselves. The fourth was dancing with a rather plump lady of mature age who was said to be extremely rich. The place was half empty: Two pretty women sat with their beaux at one table; the rest of the patrons consisted of small groups of uninteresting teenagers who didn't rate so much as a glance from our allegedly youth-possessed radio stars.

"Is it always like this?" we asked, exulting over what we found.

"Unfortunately," growled Gerd, our resident lady-killer, whereupon he lapsed into an angry tirade that obviously relieved him: For two weeks, he said, he had wasted his time in these joints. He had had enough and, from tomorrow on, he would concentrate on the guests at the hotel where we were staying.

He did just that. In a surprisingly short time he found exactly what he was looking for: a dark-haired, former ballet dancer from Milan. She was well off, married, with two nearly grown children, and a husband who had not come with her. Gerd, who was just twenty-nine and knew not one word of Italian, fell madly in love with the lady. From the day he first set eyes on Daniella, we hardly ever saw him, except, of course, when he was at the studio working. Immediately after lunch he would get up, put his arms around his girlfriend's waist, and, exchanging transfixed glances, they would step into the elevator. Sometimes they both appeared at supper, but for the most part they were simply gone.

He showed up at the station for his early shift with dark circles under his eyes, and always at the last possible moment. He couldn't praise Daniella enough. Even though she didn't speak a word of German, and his Italian was practically non-existent, he was thrilled to have finally found a woman who for the first time in his life allowed him—as he put it—to "prove his manhood," a woman who made demands, who admitted she desired him.

Even after Daniella left, the flame continued to burn (although Gerd began to console himself shortly thereafter). Daniella called regularly from Milan, and the conversations, which consisted mainly of endearing exclamations in broken German, English, or French were endless.

Then some new guests arrived: Three lively young secretaries from Berlin, with flowing hair and an inexhaustible wardrobe of bikinis; two couples from Trieste; a thin, super-elegant Italian lady with an equally thin, elegant Afghan that she brushed every day; an older Roman lawyer with a silver Lancia; and a brunette schoolteacher from Udine who was in her mid-forties and had a figure like a lady wrestler.

On the first evening Gerd sought to console himself over his separation from Daniella by taking out all three of the girls from Berlin. He was back shortly after midnight and sat down with us on the terrace without saying a word. The second day he wandered, broodingly, up and down the hotel foyer. On the third day we found him sitting in the swing with . . . who else? The teacher.

But from that point on there was no doubt in his mind.

217

For him the "superwoman" was the mature Italian. "The mature woman who knows what it's all about," he used to announce. "Such a woman has sex appeal, dignity. Next to her, the rest can get lost."

What does this show? That it's stupid to plunge into a deep depression when men rave over blonde teenagers. You have to find out what they really mean. You have to learn to differentiate between words and reality.

If you want to lose your fear of growing older, you have to force yourself to think critically. You have to keep a watchful eye on those things the media—film and television in particular—beam at us. Rule number one is that you must never forget that most movies depict fantasies, not reality. Of course there are exceptions, but what does the run-of-the-mill movie portray? The overwhelming majority deal with one man's concept of the world and are his attempt to inflict his concepts on us. Most film directors are men and, since men are usually more unsure of themselves sexually (more about that later), they create films that make them feel better, films for themselves and the rest of the males in the population. Time and again you see on the screen an older man surrounded by two or three beautiful and admiring young women, but the nature of the attraction is seldom explained. The director doesn't feel it's worth the trouble. He's not interested in truth but in daydreams and fantasy.

A typical example of more recent vintage is the mindless TV series "Charlie's Angels" and a poor French imitation shown on European television as "Charlie and His Two Beauties." Here's a typical storyline:

Charlie operates a market stand. He is short, rather unattractive, about fifty. He meets two young girls fresh out of school and hires them to work in his stand. Scarcely two minutes into the film, the director goes to the heart of the matter: The two of them naturally both fall head over heels in love with Charlie, and the dialogue hammers this into the poor viewer (as the story itself is too weak). "Do you like him?" one asks the other. "Yes, he's really out of sight," the second one says. Coming to the point, she asks, "Would you sleep with him?" There's a pause, in order to catch the viewer's attention. But don't worry, the director doesn't leave us hanging. "Certainly, right away," is the liberated answer. "Charlie is a real man."

He acts like it, too. The next scene takes place in a discothèque filled with young people. Charlie dances with the brunette, who is his favorite. The blonde, in the meantime, is left sitting by herself on the sidelines. What does she do? She wards off all attempts by young men to get her to dance; she has eyes only for Charlie, her hero. She, too, obviously only wants a "real man."

She gets one, too. The next day she meets a bald guy at the market who makes Charlie look like a beauty. He is at least forty years her senior and sells miniature cathedrals. One glance into his mobile home and all her resistance melts. She falls madly in love with him from one second to the next, leaves her friend and Charlie, and decides to go south with him.

In the next scene she is dressed only in her slip and is serving a cold beer to the object of her lust, who is lying in a rumpled bed. Unfortunately, the baldheaded guy turns out to be a swindler, and so she leaves him. Had he been honest, however, at least according to the director, he would have been a serious contender for our young lady's heart.

That this film is made to appeal to men only is evident in the choice of the main character alone. Charlie and the cathedral hawker are types that leave women cold. In spite of this, they are cast opposite two loving and adoring young females who, unbelievable as it may seem, worship them.

Had the director only taken the trouble to turn the bald character into a person of charm, humor, or lovability, a person who had something going for him, the character and story would have been credible. But he didn't do that. Instead, he used his film as just another message vehicle: Young women fall for older men because they're "real men." As laughable as these films are, they fulfill their purpose: They make publicity for the older man–young woman combination.

If you as a woman are able to recognize this, you won't be discouraged by such films any longer. You know, real life is different. The directors, as I've already mentioned, are usually men, and they obviously sympathize more with their own kind. If their films insult and upset women, the wound is not deliberate but simply because they haven't thought of women as their public. They are only attuned to their own fantasy world as seen from their own lofty perch. The rest doesn't interest them.

Today, fortunately, thankfully, more and more films are made to appeal to women too—but we've still got a long way to go. Schooling in critical thinking remains the most important weapon in fighting the fear of aging.

The basic difference between the real and the imaginary is that you can deal with reality because you are yourself real. We are defenseless, however, against a world of fanstasy unless we have learned either to keep it in perspective or to ignore it. Remember those nude photographs discussed in chapter 2? One good way to learn to think critically is to take stock each night: *What was it today that made me afraid of getting old? Was it a film, a book, a newspaper article? Was it an off-hand remark? Was I forgetful? Did I catch my husband admiring a younger woman? Or was it something I can't quite put my finger on?* Then you go over things more carefully. If the film was the reason, you can stop and realize that this was the work of one person who wants to get his own viewpoint across. Remember: Real life is different!

The same is true of books. Books neither fall from heaven nor are they filled with holy wisdom. Nobody can force me to finish reading a book that depresses and intimidates me. Life itself demands enough of my strength. Who wants to waste precious energy with gloomy reading matter? Newspaper articles fall into the same category. Journalists, in their rush to print, often repeat old clichés and outdated ideas. Because they frequently have no time to research their stories thoroughly, they fill entire paragraphs with drugstore philosophy. The result is that prejudices remain in circulation, youth is always young and beautiful, everyone else is always old and sick, and the status quo is not threatened.

What can you do? Stop reading whatever it is that offends your good sense. Don't take what you have read too seriously. Turn the pages quickly, and then forget it.

Was it a hostile remark that upset me? If so, I have to ask myself where it came from. *Was somebody trying to get even? Did I force my partner into saying this?* If not, an excellent way of protecting yourself in the future is simply to arm yourself. Fight fire with fire.

Men are often amazingly insensitive. Why? Because they have no idea of how deeply their remarks cut. It's only when they have the same thing done to them that they become more considerate. If your escort admires a young woman on the street, the best reaction is to respond immediately with, "Yes, and her date isn't that bad either." If there is no date, settle for any young male that comes your way. "I certainly wouldn't kick that doorman out of bed," or "Look at those shoulders. Aren't they gorgeous?"

221

If you have never done this before, your date (or lover, or husband, or friend) will be stricken dumb with surprise. If he gets too upset about it, you can admit that you were simply playing a game to annoy him. He'll smile about it, true, but he won't be comfortable. Who knows? Maybe you really meant it. He felt your jab just the same.

If for a time you pay back every tactless act, every unkind remark, you'll find that the man who hurt you will reform, that you won't be treated as inconsiderately as before.

Back to the stock-taking. What about the times your memory fails you? Are they necessarily a sign of diminished mental capacity or old age? Of course not. Didn't you ever, as a child, march purposefully over to a chest and find, after you had opened it, you couldn't remember what you wanted in the first place? I'm only forty now, but this recently happened to me. For four entire hours I couldn't remember the first name of a colleague with whom I had worked in Italy for a whole summer.

When something like that happens to me I laugh and say, "Boy, am I dumb." In the same situation, my eighty-two-year-old mother says in all seriousness, "I simply can't remember things anymore; it's just my age." You have to watch out for this. You shouldn't blame everything on age. Eventually, you form the habit and everything that goes wrong will be attributed to your age: "Nobody loves me; I have no friends, people are rude to me in the shops; I never get to talk in discussions; I can't sleep at night; I have no strength to get up in the morning. . . ."

Age thus becomes a wall behind which we hide in order not to have to exert ourselves. What we forget is that the wall also isolates, and that without being aware of it we cut ourselves off from life. Putting all the blame for our failings on our age, and not on ourselves, is a dangerous game. If you catch yourself playing it, STOP now! You'll be all the happier for it in the long run.

Now for some very sound advice: Don't buy any of that geriatric talk about dying brain cells. I was all of twenty-five years old the first time I was frightened out of my wits with that theory. One of my friends, a medical student, came back from one of his lectures and declared: "Well, it's all downhill for you from now on. You're already twenty-five, and every day thousands of your brain cells die."

At first I was so amazed I was speechless. Then I laughed so hard he became angry. I couldn't do anything but laugh. I was in complete possession of my powers. I knew my intellectual life was just beginning. I was not about to be intimidated by the results of some half-baked research project. If you worry about those brain cells, you are simply wasting your time. Scientists still have very far to go. To them, the brain is the biggest mystery of all.

What we do know, however, is that the brain of a forty-year-old does indeed function better than that of a twenty-year-old, and that a sixty-year-old has more interesting things to say than a thirty-year-old. This is particularly apparent when older people go back to college: They learn more easily than younger students because they have more experience and are generally more highly motivated. And isn't that what life is all about?

Basically, it is never too late to do whatever you really want to do. You can learn to play the violin at forty, and even if you'll never become a world-famous soloist you will be good enough to play for friends and family—not to mention yourself. My brother began to play the flute at forty-two. Three years later he was giving concerts. I knew a man in college who started his studies when he was sixty. He got his PhD in history at age sixty-seven.

You can also learn to ski at seventy. In Austria there's been a ski school for seniors in the town of Ramsau in Styria for the past four years. Last year the oldest participant was seventy-nine. The courses are fully booked, and most of those who attend are novice skiers. They are taught in small classes of no more than ten students. Nobody is forced to do what he or she doesn't want to do.

In conclusion, the fear of aging is not a real dread of getting older but a fear of life itself. You feel this way most often when you're physically exhausted, when the weather gets you down, when you have a cold or a bad headache, when you're generally depressed. But don't forget, there are very bad moments in youth, too. The antidotes are the usual: visit a health spa, take a trip, get involved in something outside yourself.

One of the most important influences in our life are role models, people with whom we can identify. Every one of us knows someone who exemplifies so-called eternal youth. There's no need to envy these people or make critical comments behind their backs. What we should do is try to emulate them. You can gain strength from their examples and let them spur you on to challenges of your own.

We also have to learn to be generous, to be honestly happy over somebody else's success, and to believe in the good of humankind. The key to overcoming our fear of aging lies in being an optimist and never giving up, not even in bad times. If we work hard, we can see positive changes in ourselves overnight. Today there are plenty of women who become not only more attractive but more successful as they get older. For those among us who have no role model in our own circle of acquaintances, there are plenty in public life; you take a good look and open up. Try to imitate the most successful of these, not the losers. Avoid losers whenever you can. All they can teach you is how *not* to go about conducting your life. You can't learn anything from women who have allowed themselves to be broken by unfaithful husbands, selfish lovers, envious colleagues, tyrannical bosses, and incompetent parents. These women who look old at forty, who drink too much and can't bring themselves to start all over again, can hardly give us strength. Certainly we'll not ask them for advice.

We've all had our fill of disappointment in life. We've know bad marriages and all the rest of it. But we're not going to give up. Losers are often dangerous people, because they are jealous and want to drag you down to their own level of misery. They purposedly try to discourage you. "You'll see," they say, "just you wait. It happens to all of us. You won't be an exception." And so on and so forth. Don't argue with them, don't prove to them that *they* are the exception. Let them talk, and then you say, "That may be okay for your life but not for mine." And forget about everything they've said as fast as possible.

People who aren't too successful in life, who lose their youth long before their time, always try to make others suffer for it. They use the word "age" as a weapon to strike the more youthful, the attractive, the talented, successful, efficient among us. You must have overheard them yourself. Unattractive, badly groomed women who never were beauties in a million years brag about how irresistible they were in their youth. "Alas," they say, "age comes to all of us." The same attitude is exhibited by men, mostly in a sexual context. Those older men who are lousy lovers, who never satisfied a woman in their lives, happily put the blame on age (and frighten younger men out of their wits by doing so). But every mature woman knows: A man who is a good, sensitive lover at thirty-five will be perfectly all right at seventy, if he leads a sensible life and does not drink too much. (Drug abuse is connected to impotency, too.)

Men with sexual problems are poison for women with a complex about their age. They are merciless. If they can't make love to her, it's of course *she* who is to blame. If she is young, it's because her skin has too many pimples and her bosom is too small. If she is older, well, she obviously isn't up to it anymore. These men hate advice. "Don't tell me what I have to do in bed," they declare. "I'm all right. It's all your fault, don't you see?" And they insist you stand on your head or wear out your joints in position four hundred twenty-nine because it's the only way they can perform and because it brought them rave reviews from Lady Winterbottom in Monte Carlo in 1935!

Anyway—stay clear of these men. Whatever you do will not be good enough. Any other woman could excite them more they'll imply. If nothing works, they'll resort to scratching, beating, biting, and you'll be told you're "old-fashioned" if you object. "You think I'm over the hill, don't you?" will be their parting words to you. "Well, you're wrong. Just look at you. In five years' time, no man will even want to touch you." And they'll leave you wondering whether or not you should swallow poison.

I have a friend here in Paris who swears she can tell a good lover from a bad one by the way he eats. This is her theory: If a man shovels his food into his mouth in great haste, you can't expect consideration or affection in bed. Even more suspect are those who can't bear the sight of leftovers. They hound the waiters to wisk the plates away the moment they have finished eating. This of course, has deep psychological meaning. It shows that the man has

226

eaten with guilt and that he is not comfortable with physical pleasures. He is ashamed because he enjoyed his meal.
A man who has such a distorted relationship with his
senses can hardly be a good lover.

How, then, do you recognize a potentially talented lover?
My friend knows the answer: by all those actions that people outside of France find outright disgusting. If your man
enjoys his food openly and talks at great length about it,
if he takes ages to finish a Sunday lunch, if he snatches
dirty dishes from the waiter's hands to mop up a little left-
over gravy, if he picks choice morsels off chicken bones,
and if he kneads little pieces of bread between his fingers
on and off throughout the meal—according to my friend,
that's the man for you. I myself believe that you can tell a
good lover by the fact that he never tells a dirty joke. He
finds physical love too beautiful to diminish it with coarse
words. He knows he's good and therefore never boasts
about his prowess. And he is certainly not afraid of older
women.

A few last words about women in general. Young women
must stop making life difficult for their elders. They must
realize that everything they do to them inevitably boom-
erangs. If they make fun of women past their early youth,
they are only setting the stage for their own ridicule once
they're grown up. Many young women are insufferable in
the company of men. They develop a compulsion for being
noticed, insist on being the center of attention, and run
down everybody else in the process, all in order to shine
in a better light. Above all, they can't stand to listen to
praise of someone else. "What!" they grumble. "They're
falling all over this person who's at least fifteen years older
than I am." The fact that they themselves won't stay young
forever doesn't enter their little heads. This rivalry has to

stop. We're all in the same boat. If we think logically, every older woman's success should fill us with pride. Every compliment paid *her* today can be paid to *us* tomorrow.

Why are young people so aggressive? Why do they constantly yell: "We are young and you are old?" The answer is simple: because it is their only weapon. Young people haven't achieved anything yet. They have no experience and little knowledge. They have very few successes (if any) to look back on. They have no money. They are still dependent on adults. Youth is the only thing they have got, and it probably would not occur to them to brag about it, if adults wouldn't constantly tell them how great it is to be young.

We live in an age of great tolerance. We do not subjugate children and adolescents to the strict codes of former centuries. That's good. But we have gone a little bit too far. Let's look back. Only two generations ago, no adolescent would have dared to lecture his parents. And why should they be permitted to do it now? The parents still know much more than the children do. If they don't keep up with the latest developments on the pop scene, it's simply because this is of no importance to them. Parents usually know what counts in life. For this they must be respected.

I remember my youth very well. It really wasn't all that great. The more insecure I felt, the more aggressively I behaved. People who rave about their youth have forgotten what it was really like: complexes, extreme rivalries between classmates, gangs of boys you were scared of, baby fat, terrible fears of growing too tall (or not tall enough), agonies that your period wouldn't come and that you'd never be able to bear children.

The grown woman who says: "It used to be so easy to

find a boyfriend when I was young," doesn't remember the facts. Of course there were swarms of boys around. Schoolchildren aren't usually married. But if you remember well, the one we really wanted, we most certainly never got. The one boy we had a crush on was always in love with somebody else. And if we did get him, finally, after much effort, we discovered that he wasn't right for us after all.

The same goes for friendships. The myth that you can only make lasting friendships in your youth has long been disproven. We generally find those people who are really suited to us much later in life. Of course there are exceptions. There do indeed exist school friendships that last a lifetime. But, thinking back, who were those people we mixed with? Well, it was those with whom we were thrown together, not those we chose. We only met people from the same neighborhood, from the same school, the same dance class. The boundaries were very narrow.

As adults we have the whole world to choose from. We are free to travel, to live in different countries. We can move from city to city and make new friends wherever we go. My own circle of acquaintances had quadrupled in the past seven years, and life has become boundlessly exciting, compared to what it was in my teens. This is true not only for writers and journalists but for all of us who are in professions that bring us into close contact with people. It doesn't matter whether you're a saleswoman, doctor, secretary, hairdresser, lawyer, nurse, or architect. If you're extroverted and love people, you'll make your best friends in later life. And you'll continue making them as long as you live.

Why do so many people believe that youth is a period of constant happiness? Perhaps because, if you recall an event, you only see it in your mind's eye. You experience it unencumbered by physical circumstances. You are not aware of your own body, for example, as you normally would be. Reliving an event from the past, you are not disturbed by inconveniences—like a grain of sand in your eye, shoes that pinched, a cut on your finger, a toothache, a headache, that terrible feeling of insecurity when you knew you were overweight or when your hairstyle wasn't right—all those things that weighed upon you and put a damper on your general state of well-being.

Secondly, in recalling events, we leave out most of the psychological problems that attended them. We recall a nice party, for example, *without* remembering the anxiety about being asked in the first place, the ill-timed outbreak of acne, the apprehensions over final exams the following week, the worries over a sick father, or whether or not college applications would meet with success.

Finally, we view the past with a certain feeling of relief, of security, because we have *survived* all those situations. Because of this, we feel secure. And, looking back, we mistakenly believe that we felt just as safe then.

Everybody should keep a diary in order to put things into perspective. A diary helps us find out just how "carefree" our youth really was. You need not fill complete pages every night but a few notes in a small pocket calendar are enough to bring back the picture of how things really were ten, even twenty years ago. I have kept diaries since I was eighteen years old and therefore have no illusions about my "glorious" youth. On the contrary, reading about myself and my life so many years ago, I'm almost ashamed how naïve, how blind, and how stupid I was. I'll give you an example. When I was twenty-four years old, I found myself in Australia. I had traveled from Paris to Marseille and then by boat to Sydney via Egypt, India, Ceylon, and Singapore. In Sydney I ran out of money and had to earn my fare back home by working for an import-export firm.

A Czech woman named Anna worked for the same company and I liked her from the start; she was attractive and full of fun. After a few days I finally worked up enough courage to ask one of our fellow workers about Anna, and it was then that I learned her age. I was struck dumb. Anna was thirty-three years old!

I simply couldn't believe it. I myself was twenty-four and a willing victim of the youth cult and fear of aging. I had been told that thirty-three was old. The mere number made me feel very uncomfortable. As a result, I began to look at Anna with suspicion. When I saw her striding happily to the bus stop after work, young and jaunty in her little green hat, I could only think: *This can't be true!*

Obviously, my brain was not yet functioning properly. I was not capable of telling myself: *Anna is the living proof that thirty-three is young. We have been deceived. Society has placed false standards before us. We must change this. Citizens, to arms!* No, nothing like that. Instead, I started looking closely to see whether Anna had wrinkles or any other signs of age. I found none. Her skin was lovely, her eyes sparkling with good humor. Still, I wasn't convinced. I simply didn't understand the world anymore. Had I lived in the Middle Ages and had Anna been charged with witchcraft, I would have yelled along with the others at the top of my lungs: "She's a witch, a witch!"

So much for my state of mind at twenty-four, which at that time I would have defended as wholly sound and sensible. As uncertain, young, and stupid I was, I was also arrogant. Youth was my only security.

In September 1978 the American actor Robert Mitchum came to Austria to film *Steiner II*. He had just passed sixty and had promised to give me an interview if I came to an army training camp near Wels in upper Austria where the film was being shot. When I arrived the whole army base smelled of incense that was being burned to simulate clouds of smoke from a nearby battlefield. Mitchum was in a jeep, driving up and down "the front." Tanks and soldiers where everywhere.

I spent the whole day on location and found time enough to ask Mitchum what he thought of the youth cult in the United States. (Mitchum is a fascinating storyteller once you've survived the initial onslaught of four-letter words!) Anyway, the youth cult did not concern Mitchum in the least. He knows what he is worth and he feels threatened by nobody. Besides, he said, the whole youth-cult thing is a pure business deal. For the first time in American history young people have had money to spare, and that's the only reason we go out of our way to please them. "Blue jeans and John Travolta," he commented, "brought in a few additional million dollars. That's the whole secret; it's not a question of who is worth more, the young or old. Believe me, an advertising campaign could kill the youth cult over night."

Mitchum is right. Even though words like "young and swinging" have gained in importance, the facts haven't changed. Power still lies with the adult and, to overwhelming degrees, with those over fifty. There are, of course, young millionaires, young general managers, and even a club of "young presidents" (for those who have made it to the top of their companies before the age of forty). However, the majority of those who really have something to say, whether in politics, business, science, or the arts, are over fifty. Every grown-up who is afraid of young people should remember this.

Speaking of being afraid, life is too short to poison it with fears, in particular with the fear of getting older. Fear is dreadful. It leads to misunderstandings between people who love one another, to fights and wars, to aggression at home and misery and intrigues at the office. Fear can kill people at the pinnacle of their lives. The most beautiful sentence in the Bible says, "Fear not."

Let me tell you about an interesting encounter I had at a publishing party that was held in a very fashionable Viennese art gallery. Radio and TV personalities were there, all the "beautiful people" came, and the three floors of the building were packed with elegant men and exquisitely dressed women. It was practically impossible to find a seat (or a quiet corner), but I was lucky. I discovered a black leather sofa in a pretty niche behind the main staircase, and there was still room on it. I sat down, delighted, and started talking to my neighbor, who was a dignified-looking older woman with a very kind face. I liked her right away, particularly because she did not let all the commotion make her nervous. She smiled to herself, sipping her orange juice mixed with champagne, and we were soon talking together as if we had known each other all our lives.

It turned out that she was a very wealthy German who had recently bought a big castle north of Vienna and was renovating it at enormous cost. My first question was, "Aren't you afraid of the political situation in Austria? After all, we are right at the Iron Curtain. Can you chance that kind of investment? Aren't you scared?"

Her answer impressed me very much. "No, my child," she smiled, "I am not. I have stopped being afraid altogether. I am too old now to be afraid of anything." (She was barely sixty.) It was as if my eyes were open for the first time. I saw the light. *"Good heavens,"* I remember thinking, *"she's right.* How much time do we waste being afraid of things that never happen? Or that, when they do happen, are not half as bad as we had feared? How easy

233

it is to be afraid all the time. It is much easier then being courageous, optimistic, prepared to fight. Life would be so much more enjoyable if we could only consolidate our strength and say: "From now on, I won't be scared. I'm too old to be afraid."

This is especially so for people suffering from age fright. Once you decide not to be afraid of your age anymore— *never, ever again*— you've done yourself a very good turn. And you'll ask: "Why didn't I do it sooner?" You'll feel so relieved. Everything will seem so clear and easy. On the other hand, if you don't work hard to shake off your fear, it might become so strong that it will dominate your whole existence. Such fear is similar to depression: Once it has reached a certain depth, it becomes a vicious circle and you're trapped for good. Unconsciously you do everything you can *not* to come out of it. Don't let yourself go that far. Learn to appreciate what you have, enjoy the advantages each stage in your life will bring you, and take pleasure in everyday things.

Most important: Don't let fear of some future event spoil the great pleasure of *looking forward to something*. Everyone of us has looked forward to birthdays or holidays that didn't turn out as we had hoped. That's part of the game, I suppose. But you must not make the mistake of saying: "I've been disappointed before, so I won't look forward to anything anymore." This is ridiculous. And, in doing so, you'll rob yourself of many very agreeable moments, pleasant thoughts, in short, of a good time. You should and you *must* anticipate pleasure if you want to go through this world and stay sane. Never let fear triumph. There's enough time for fear once the dreaded event happens. But, strangely enough, most catastrophes hit us out of the blue, and if they do, you'll be amazed how strong you suddenly

234

are, how quickly you can adjust if you have to. Life goes on. And, believe me, it goes on much better without fear.

One last example for those who still believe that in old age you necessarily must be feeble. Not long ago, I was looking over some travel brochures put out by a firm specializing in "adventure holidays" to the Far East. I was especially interested in a trip to the Philippines; it sounded very exciting and out of the ordinary. The tour went to coral islands; to famous, hidden temples in the jungle; to the area's oldest stone church, built by the Spanish conquerors; to the smallest volcano on earth; and, of course, to the world-famous rice terrace, the "stairway to heaven."

I called the travel agent and asked for more details. I was particularly interested in the rice terrace. "It's an hour's flight from Manila," a friendly lady on the other end of the telephone said, "and you reach the first field after a relatively short walk. If you really want to see the very famous ones on top of the mountain, then you have to walk three hours through the jungle."

I asked whether or not the other tour participants were ready to do this, and she replied, "No problem, dear, we'll walk all right. We have several old ladies in the group." Then she sensed my surprise and added, "You would have no way of knowing, but for us in the travel business it's a well-known fact that older people exert themselves much more than the young ones. Our old ladies are passionate walkers. They'll tramp through the jungle with a vengeance. Two eighty-year-olds have signed on for our New Guinea trip. We're happy to have them. They won't complain about mosquito bites or spending a night in a sleeping bag. Give me an old lady anytime. They're never any trouble."

235

So why be afraid? Let's be happy to be alive, and happy that we get older. Stick to positive role models and give your very best. Living is like dancing. If you do it well, you'll never have to worry. For years dancing was regarded as something only young people did. If a child wanted to study ballet, someone would always say: "And what will you do when you're forty?"

Now this prejudice is waning. Margot Fonteyn, probably the most famous dancer of our time, is over sixty and still dancing. The prima ballerina of the Bolshoi Ballet, Maya Plisetskaya, was born in 1924 and is still dancing. I've already mentioned Martha Graham, the founder of modern dance, who was still on stage at eighty.

Dancing is like life. The person who has little patience usually does not last long. Poorly trained dancers are always accident prone. They may land incorrectly after a jump and injure their spine, knees, or ankles. At the age of forty they may be relegated to the dance studio.

A well-trained dancer is in top form. Rudolf Nureyev was in top form at forty. And, if he feels up to it, at fifty and sixty he'll still be dancing. Because, as everyone in the field tells you, the beauty of dance is in the expression, and this comes only with maturity.

Maturity is the essence of life. Nothing can make up for it, not even the prettiest face. We live in a demanding age: We want content not appearances. We do not believe in statements; we want a logical explanation. We no longer trust blindly. Outdated prejudices have no place in our world. Times have changed. We know that we are better now than we were at twenty. A new era has begun, a freer, more tolerant one.

And it belongs to the mature woman.

How did actress Susan Strasberg put it to reporters? "When I was young," she said, "I lived with blinders on.

I never saw the options that I had. Now life is a great adventure . . . I compare myself to a bottle of wine—the older I get, the better I'll be. By the time I'm ninety, I'll be just about ready to be decanted. God willing, I'm going to be one hell of a terrific old lady!"